PUTTING WOMEN IN THEIR PLACE

SMYTH&HELWYS
PUBLISHING, INCORPORATED   MACON, GEORGIA

PUTTING WOMEN
In Their Place

Moving Beyond
Gender Stereotypes
in Church and Home

Edited by
AUDRA and
JOE TRULL

Smyth & Helwys Publishing, Inc.
6316 Peake Road
Macon, Georgia 31210-3960
1-800-747-3016

Library of Congress Cataloging-in-Publication Data

Putting women in their place : moving beyond gender stereotypes
in church and home /
[edited by] Joe E. Trull and Audra E. Trull.
p. cm.
ISBN 1-57312-409-5
1. Women—Religious aspects—Southern Baptist Convention.
2. Southern Baptist Convention—Doctrines.
I. Trull, Joe E.
II Trull, Audra E., 1937-
BX6462.7 .P88 2003
261.8'343'088261—dc21

2002152737

CONTENTS

PREFACE

In the early 1800s, Texas was a frontier territory. One historian noted that settlers believed "Indians were to be killed, African Americans were to be enslaved, and Hispanics were to be avoided." In the 1830s these "Texicans" built a Baptist church at Independence that had two doors: one for white males and the other for "women and other creatures."[1]

Female subjugation is not new—it began in the early chapters of Genesis. Serious debate about female equality is more recent. In modern history, the founding mothers of the feminist movement in this country wrote, spoke, and marched from the 1840s to the 1940s. During the last half-century, the voice of feminism has become more diverse and much louder. People are listening. Much has changed.

Religious groups often have been at the forefront of the call for female equality in American life. In contrast, perhaps nowhere has female discrimination and subordination been more obvious than in churches, especially the more conservative denominations like the Southern Baptist Convention (SBC). During the last decade a wide variety of evangelicals have organized and petitioned for female equality in both church and home life, basing their convictions on a clearer understanding of biblical equality.

In the year 2003, Baptists (especially Southern Baptists) are still ambivalent about which "doors" women should be allowed to enter! As was true in the twentieth-century debate about racial segregation and discrimination, Baptists tend to be among the last to realize and admit that their beliefs are too often fashioned by the surrounding culture more than by their Christian faith. In regards to both racial and gender equality, Baptists have used selected "proof-texts" from the Bible to defend the status quo.[2]

The overarching purpose of this book is to provide readers (both Baptists and others) with an introduction to the present debate among Southern Baptists over female equality. This text may serve as a primer, for it is written with the understanding that many of our readers will be exploring the various aspects of female equality for the first time. We hope many laypeople and churches will discover this book to be a helpful and enlightening text.

At the same time, although some of the chapters are first-person responses to events, a majority of the articles are serious studies of the biblical, theological, and historical aspects of the debate. College and seminary students will discover these chapters do not lack in biblical, theological, or intellectual depth.

One glance at the paragraph descriptions of each author's history and credentials will impress even the most critical reader. They are a diverse group of prolific writers: pastors, college teachers, seminary professors, editors, and renowned scholars. All are knowledgeable and responsible Baptist thinkers who understand Baptist ways. Each one brings a special understanding of the subject she or he addresses.

In the introduction, the editors provide a basic understanding of the background for the present debate, including the recent history of the feminist movement and the rise of Christian feminism. Essential to the Baptist controversy is the significant impact of the takeover of the SBC by conservative resurgents, which resulted in SBC resolutions and drastic revisions of the *Baptist Faith and Message* document concerning the proper place for women in church and home.

The first four chapters record personal responses to recent SBC declarations concerning the place of women in the church and home by a renowned theologian-preacher, a female pastor, a long-time Baptist educator, and a former SBC missionary.

Chapters 5 through 8 discuss biblical insights into the issue with chapters on biblical authority, women leaders in the Bible, the revolutionary example of Jesus, and the often misunderstood position of Paul the Apostle concerning women.

Chapter 9 examines a serious and complex theological question: how does our sexuality relate to the nature of God? Chapters 10 through 12 address the practical issues of authority and submission in the home, female leadership in the church, and the calling and ordination of women ministers.

Four of the chapters in this book (1, 3, 4, and 5) were originally published in the bimonthly journal *Christian Ethics Today,* and are reprinted by permission.[3] Unless otherwise indicated, the version of the Bible quoted within is the NRSV.[4] Chapter 3 also appears in Charles Wellborn's book *Grits, Grace, and Goodness* (Smyth & Helwys, 2003).

A project such as this requires inspiration, outside expertise, and professional guidance. This book has been inspired by many individuals, both women and men, who have shared our vision for female equality in Baptist life. Many, like Shannon and Renate, were students at New Orleans seminary. Others, like Deborah and Oda Lisa, are members of our church and remind us weekly that Phoebe and Priscilla are still with us. We are inspired the most by a host of colleagues—teachers, missionaries, pastors, denominational workers, and a band of faithful believers—who have suffered personally and vocationally because of their refusal to compromise their beliefs about gender equality.

Ever since a chance meeting with Catherine Kroeger in New Orleans years ago, we have benefited from her rich knowledge and the vast resources of the organization she founded—Christians for Biblical Equality.[5] More specifically, this book is a labor of love by the authors of each chapter, each of whom is sharing a lifetime of dedicated study and service.

Finally, we wish to thank Keith Gammons, Kelley Land, and Jessica Ellison at Smyth & Helwys Publishing for their guidance and assistance in helping us to pull it all together.

In light of the present divisions in Baptist life, our great hope is the one uttered by a Puritan divine: "There may yet be more truth to break forth from God's Word." +

NOTES

[1] Cited in a news story, *Baptist Standard,* 16 June 1993, 3.

[2] See chapter 8, "Human Equality—Gender and Race," in Joe E. Trull, *Walking in the Way: An Introduction to Christian Ethics* (Nashville: Broadman & Holman, 1997).

[3] The journal is available free of charge to subscribers through the website at <www.ChristianEthicsToday.com> or by contacting the editor at jtrull@wimberley-tx.com.

[4] New Revised Standard Version, copyright 1989, Division of Christian Education of the National Council of the Churches of Christ in the USA.

[5] The organization may be contacted at 122 W. Franklin Ave., Suite 218, Minneapolis, MN 55404 or on their website at <www.cbeinternational.org>.

How Baptists Got Into This Debate

Audra E. Trull and Joe E. Trull

The summer of 2000 was a crucial turning point for both of us. After fifteen years of teaching Christian ethics and working with students at a Baptist seminary, we returned to Texas to begin a new phase of our lives, one we had not anticipated (more about that later).[1]

One afternoon the telephone rang. On the line was Penny, the wife of a former seminary student. She had difficulty speaking as she asked, "What did I do wrong?"

At the seminary where we first met the couple, Penny was invited to join the first group of females to receive a new degree in women's ministries. After the first year of study, an opportunity arose for Penny to serve for a week as a chaplain on a cruise line—"a time of ministry I shall never forget." Upon returning to the campus and sharing her experiences aboard the ship, her major professor (a female) called her aside privately.

Gently but firmly Penny was told never to serve as a "Cruise Chaplain" again! Why? No woman should occupy such a role—this was a position for a man. In addition, she had brought embarrassment to the seminary, for the Southern Baptist Convention (SBC) meeting in their city that very month had approved a document forbidding female pastors.[2] She was further warned never to discuss this matter with anyone—professors, students, or other ministers.

As best we could over the phone, we gave Penny our comfort and counsel. We also directed her to an organization that provided support and information for women in ministry who faced opposition. In time she was able to write her own account of the incident, which was published by that organization under the title "Woman Overboard."[3]

Penny's repeated question remains with us to this day: "What did I do wrong?" The summer of 2000 was for her a crucial turning point.

That same summer was also a watershed moment for Southern Baptists. Like a perfect storm, the takeover of the SBC by ultra-conservatives had reached maximum intensity. By the year 2000, faculties and curriculums at theological schools were drastically changed. Mission agencies had revised their purposes, restructured their programs, and reassigned missionaries. Denominational agencies had reorganized under new mandates. Churches that assumed the squabble was a "preacher fight" suddenly realized the short- and long-term effects of the takeover were impacting their congregations. And along the path of the storm where the winds were strongest, scores of victims lay injured and bleeding—presidents and professors, missions board leaders and missionaries, agency heads and staff members, editors and secretaries, and many innocent bystanders like Penny.

THE TAKEOVER OF THE SBC

For the largest Protestant denomination in the U.S., the summer of 2000 marked the culmination of twenty years of religious warfare between two groups. In the late 1970s a well-organized and well-financed cadre of ultra-conservatives launched a plan to gain control of the SBC. Moderate Baptists at first were reluctant to engage in this battle that resembled secular politics more than religion. When they did organize opposition, it was too late.

The strategy worked. By the 1990s the takeover was complete, as the organizers had put themselves into positions of leadership and control in the SBC. During the last decade of the twentieth century the leaders of this "conservative resurgence" (as they called it) relished their victory and immediately began the radical change of every institution and agency under their direction.[4]

In order to solidify their political successes, SBC leaders began rewriting the convention's history from their perspective and rewriting the convention's faith statement, *The Baptist Faith and Message* (*BF&M*) to reflect their narrow fundamentalist-conservative beliefs.

Although this twenty-year struggle for control had many faces and numerous issues, in recent years one subject has become the focal point of debate—female equality. The two most significant revisions of the *BF&M*, one in 1998 and one in 2000, focused on the role of women in the home and in the church. High-profile personalities who were instrumental in the takeover engineered the controversial revisions in this SBC confession of faith, which had served the convention for 153 years. According to the former President of Southwestern Baptist Theological Seminary, Russell H. Dilday, "This revised statement of faith . . . is being used as an official creed to enforce loyalty to the party in power. To refuse is to risk isolation or even expulsion from the denominational circle."[5]

One issue became the major test of orthodoxy—how a person or a congregation understood gender roles determined doctrinal soundness. To believe contrary to the *2000 BF&M* statement was to deny the "inerrancy of the Bible," so the revisers claimed.

THE STRUGGLE FOR FEMALE EQUALITY

This battle over female equality did not begin with Baptists or even with Gloria Steinem. From the earliest chapters of Genesis, the devaluation of females has been a constant story in human history. Patriarchy, male domination, discrimination, and sexism have characterized almost every civilization.

The Greek myth of Amazon female warriors who ruled a society in Scythia is pure fantasy. Also idealistic was Plato's just state composed of three social classes of equal people. The reality is that in every society, including Plato's Greek state, women have been treated as second-class citizens, sometimes not much more than disposable property or worthless slaves.[6]

Only since the twentieth century has complete equality for women come close to realization. In the United States, women gained the right to vote in 1920. Today they are elected as mayors, governors, senators, and Supreme Court justices. Sixty years ago women were called into the workforce to aid their country during World War II. Today, career women work in almost every vocation. Five decades ago, women in America had no guarantee of equal access to employment, housing, education, or credit. Today these rights are established by law.

In this past century, a dramatic reversal has occurred in society's attitude toward the abuse of females. In language and in law, in business and in family life, sexual harassment and the mistreatment of women have become major concerns. The plight of oppressed Afghan women has increased American awareness of this world problem.

In light of the twentieth-century emancipation of women from domination, discrimination, and sexism, where does the church stand? Have not Christian beliefs and practices sometimes perpetuated female subordination? Has the church been more prone to uphold social customs and cultural traditions concerning women than to declare and support God's creative intent for female and male relationships?

THE RESPONSE OF CHURCHES TO CHRISTIAN
FEMINIST MOVEMENTS

As we enter the third millennium, few topics have generated more heated discussion among both Protestants and Roman Catholics than gender roles and relationships. Feminist studies are common in theological schools, with no shortage of books and articles for the bibliography. Feminist theology is the topic of conferences, as well as a major "bone of contention" in many denominations. No one denies the important role of women in the family and in the religious community. At the same time, traditional understandings of female roles, usually supported by biblical passages, have often placed women in a secondary position and deprived them of full involvement. Today, as never before, Christians are debating the proper place for women.

Evangelicals have carried on a friendly but serious dispute on this subject for more than fifteen years. In 1990, the Evangelical Theological Society (ETS) held their annual meeting on the New Orleans Seminary campus. Members of this group are known to be conservative scholars who hold a high view of Scripture. As we browsed in their display area, we discovered two groups promoting opposing views of male and female roles. Leaders in both circles were well-known theologians who based their views on the biblical revelation, and who (unlike many Baptists) were able to discuss their convictions with candor and mutual respect.

At one table marked Christians for Biblical Equality (CBE) sat Catherine Kroeger, an expert in the ancient Greek language, classical Greek literature, and the Graeco-Roman culture of the first century. As a minister's wife and foster mother of numerous children, she returned to the University of Minnesota late in life to earn her doctorate in the classics, convinced that many traditional understandings of gender were based on a faulty interpretation of the Bible in its first-century setting. Through research, writing, and speaking, Dr. Kroeger has expanded our knowledge of the New Testament world and of biblical teachings concerning females (see chapter 8, "Paul: Supporter and Exhorter of Women"). In 1987 she founded CBE, "an organization of Christians who believe the Bible, properly interpreted, teaches the fundamental equality of men and women of all racial and ethnic groups, all economic classes, and all age groups."[7]

At a second table at the ETS meeting was a representative of the Council on Biblical Manhood and Womanhood (CBMW), established for the purpose of "studying and setting forth biblical teachings on the relationship between men and women, especially in the home and church." The council was formed in 1987, in response to CBE, to clear up the "confusion about male and female roles in the Christian world today" and to affirm that "God made men and women equal in personhood and in value, but different in roles."[8]

At the first CBMW meeting, leaders in the group developed "The Danvers Statement," a declaration of the organization's rationale, purposes, and affirmations, published in final form in November 1988.[9] In 1991 this traditionalist group published a 566-page book of twenty-six essays, significantly subtitled *A Response to Evangelical Feminism.*[10]

As evangelicals debated the meaning of biblical teachings on gender issues,[11] the World Council of Churches called mainline denominations to a decade-long (1988–1998) focus on women. A central element in the feminist emphasis was the need for God, the community, and the church to be "re-imagined."

A RE-Imagining conference in the fall of 1993 brought together two thousand participants representing thirty-two denominations and twenty-seven countries. Most conferees represented the "gender feminist" perspective, rallying around key themes of women's suffrage, male patriarchy, sexism by the traditional Christian church, and the need to reinterpret the Bible and its teachings.

Few would deny that feminism has played a major role in bringing full equality to twenty-first-century women. Many Baptists, however, fail to distinguish between the founding mothers of feminism who wrote and worked for equality from the 1840s to 1940s and the various contemporary expressions of the movement. Today there is pluralism within feminism. In the 1960s and 1970s a radical feminist ethic emerged that taught that the only way to alleviate women's plight was to achieve total autonomy—political, economic, sexual, and reproductive freedom, either through separation or seizing power from men.[12]

Many contemporary theologians have noted a split in the Christian feminist movement. The more radical "gender feminist" theologians emphasize the meaning of femaleness and the need to "re-imagine" traditional beliefs,[13] while "equity feminism" affirms orthodox Christianity is essentially correct but needs structural reform to achieve equality, civil rights, and an end to discrimination. This distinction is crucial for Baptists, who tend to lump all movements for female equality into the radical feminist category. Such stereotyping is at best naïve, and at worst intentionally deceptive and misleading.

THE BAPTIST DEBATE OVER FEMALE EQUALITY

How does this brief overview of the struggle for female equality during the last century, and particularly its impact on American religious life, relate to the present Baptist controversy? As we have noted, the powers-that-be who control today's SBC have consolidated their dominance, using the *1998 Family Amendment* and the *2000 BF&M* statement and its pronouncements on women as a line of demarcation for passing the muster of "doctrinal accountability."[14] In a word, if you don't put women in their assigned place (so say SBC leaders), we will put you in your place—outside the boundaries of orthodoxy and partnership.

In order to understand the present Baptist debate over female equality, we need to look briefly at the SBC record concerning female equality, and then we will examine closely three documents that ignited this present firestorm. The debate over the place of women in Baptist life did not begin with the recent takeover movement. The issue was argued even before the beginning of the SBC in 1845. Four decades later, in 1885, two women from Arkansas tried to register as voting messengers to the SBC annual meeting. This attempt triggered a change in the wording of the SBC constitution regarding who could be seated as voting messengers, from "members" to "brethren." Not until 1918 was the change reversed, but this was still two years before women in the U.S. were given the right to vote.[15]

In an article in the *Encyclopedia of Southern Baptists* published in 1958, Juliette Mather identified a major flaw in the SBC. Noting the financial support of missions stimulated by the Women's Missionary Union and the large number of women leaders serving in local churches, she expressed disappointment that females had been largely overlooked as denominational leaders.[16]

Coinciding with the publication of *The Feminine Mystic* in 1963, the SBC elected its first woman officer, Marie Mathis of Texas, as second vice president. In the same year that the Equal Rights Amendment was passed (1972), Marie Mathis was nominated for president of the SBC—the only woman so nominated to date—but she was defeated.[17]

The 1984 Resolution. The 1984 convention meeting in Kansas City signaled a radical change in SBC attitudes toward women. The conservative leaders who began the takeover of the SBC in 1979 fueled the heated debate over female leadership by sponsoring a strongly worded resolution opposing ordination of women, which passed by a vote of 4793 to 3466.[18] Resolution Three took the position that the Bible excludes women from pastoral leadership positions, concluding: "We encourage the service of women in all aspects of church life and work other than pastoral functions and leadership roles entailing ordination." Even more inflammatory was the written justification given for the action: this rule was to "preserve a submission that God requires because man was first in Creation, and woman was first in the Edenic Fall."[19]

Reaction was vigorous and varied. To proclaim male superiority based on the supposed chronology of Genesis was widely challenged as poor exegesis. To blame Eve for original sin in the Garden of Eden, which resulted in a penalty upon all females, exposed the superficial theology of the Resolutions Committee. But Pandora's Box had been opened. A lively debate about the origin of sin ensued, often including Paul's statement in Romans 5:12, "Sin came into the world through one *man*."

One year earlier, a group of SBC women had met in Louisville, Kentucky, to begin the formation of a new organization: Southern Baptist Women in Ministry.[20] The 1984 resolution seemed to energize this new association (now renamed Baptist Women in Ministry), which immediately became a rallying force in opposition to the SBC attempt to limit female leadership. In 2002 over 1900 women serve as ordained Southern Baptist clergy, mostly as chaplains and staff members. Ironically, the majority of them received their ordination after 1984.[21]

Article XVIII: The 1998 Family Amendment. The 1984 Resolution was a harbinger of things to come. A key concern of the new leadership in the SBC was to establish a very definite role for women—to put them in their "assigned" place at home and in the church. The new leaders of the SBC had always held a traditionalist view about women. But now, the gender issue seemed a perfect tool for ostracizing and eliminating their moderate Baptist opponents. Two SBC power brokers, Richard Land (Ethics and Religious Liberty Commission President and a member of both the 1998 and 2000 committees) and Paige Patterson (Southeastern Seminary president) had been dean and president of the ultra-conservative Criswell School of Theology. Patterson's wife Dorothy was appointed to the 1998 committee. As newly elected SBC President, Patterson in turn appointed the 2000 committee, which included his brother-in-law, New Orleans Seminary President Chuck Kelley.

Recent SBC President Adrian Rogers (Chair of the 2000 Committee) and his wife Joyce, along with Paige and Dorothy Patterson, were original board members of the traditionalist Council on Biblical Manhood and Womanhood. Al Mohler, the young Southern Seminary president, was also appointed to the *2000 BF&M* committee, following his wife Mary Mohler's role as one of seven on the 1998 committee. Is it any surprise that this core group would draw some very specific boundary lines about women's roles?

Article XVIII, an Amendment to the *1963 BF&M* document, is titled "The Family" and consists of a four-paragraph (272 words) statement accompanied by a twenty-paragraph commentary.[22] On first reading, the brief statement (followed by a long list of supportive scriptures) seems "thoroughly biblical" and innocuous to the casual reader. Paragraphs one and two affirm the family and the purposes of marriage. The last paragraph discusses the parent-child relationship.

The controversial third paragraph reads:

> The husband and wife are of equal worth before God. Both bear God's image *but in differing ways.* The marriage relationship models the way God relates to his people. A husband is to love his wife as Christ loved the church. He has the *God-given responsibility to provide for, to protect, and to lead the family. A wife is to submit graciously to the servant leadership of her husband* even as the church willingly submits to the headship of Christ. She, being 'in the image of God' as is her husband and thus equal to him, has the *God-given responsibility to respect her husband and serve as his "helper" in managing their household and nurturing the next generation.*

The italicized phrases need closer examination. It is obvious upon a second look that the committee of seven intended to define very specific male and female roles in the home. Traditionalists love to utter the oxymoronic idea that men and women are "equal . . . but in different ways." As gender issue scholar Rebecca Merrill Groothius has noted in an extensive article on this subject, "The idea that women are equal in their being, yet unequal by virtue of their being, simply makes no sense."[23]

Note the subtle but definite assignment of "God-given" roles: men are responsible "to provide for, to protect, and to lead the family." In other words, the husband alone is to work outside the home and to be in charge as the guardian of the family. On the other hand, the wife's "God-given" responsibility is to "submit graciously" to her husband's leadership, to "respect" him and "serve as his 'helper' in managing" the household and "nurturing" the children. In other words, the wife is ordained by God to remain in the home primarily to pay the bills, cook the meals, clean the house, and raise the kids.

Now, all of these family tasks are important. But the obvious problem with such boundaries is the assumption that the husband has little or no responsibility to nurture the children, manage the home, or help the wife with household tasks. Likewise, the subtle implication for the wife and mother is that she should not work outside the home or consider herself a provider, protector, or leader of the family. In this description of gender roles we have a solid basis for "Men Only" in the pastorate.

The greatest repercussions to the *Family Amendment* came from the phrase "A wife is to submit graciously to the servant leadership of her husband," based primarily on a flawed exegesis of Ephesians 5:21-25 (see chapter 10 for an extensive discussion of this passage). Though traditionalists claim to be "biblical," the word "graciously" is nowhere in the passage. Does this additional adverb mean that wives must *not* say, "Okay, I'll do it," and frown, but rather they must smile and be sweet as they submit?

Dorothy Patterson was questioned by a reporter about female submission in the amendment she helped frame. "As a woman standing under the authority of Scripture, even when it comes to submitting to my husband when I know he's wrong, I just have to do it and then he stands accountable at the judgment," she replied.[24] Think about that statement. For a wife to claim that she is not accountable to God for a decision required by her husband, but only he is responsible, is close to theological heresy! This viewpoint contends either the husband knows best, or if not, he alone will answer to God.

This hierarchical view of marriage, made popular by Bill Gothard's "Chain of Command" model, has authority flowing from God to Husband to Wife to Children. Many wives love this approach because it relieves them of responsibility. As the family leader, the husband is the one accountable to God for the family, while the wife is accountable to her husband. We have now in this theory an ironic reversal of the traditionalist interpretation of the fall, where Eve and women are blamed for sin.

The 2000 BF&M. The leaders of the SBC were unrelenting in their quest for "doctrinal uniformity." They seemed determined to exclude all Southern Baptists who do not agree with them on certain key issues, a major one being the role of women. Two years after the *Family Amendment*, a fifteen-member committee (appointed the previous summer by SBC President Paige Patterson) released proposed revisions to the *1963 BF&M*. The SBC meeting in New Orleans in June approved the *2000 BF&M*. Numerous changes troubled large numbers of Baptist leaders across the convention. In a compelling and well-documented analysis of the *2000 BF&M*, the former president of the SBC's largest seminary summarized eleven major concerns about the revision, including the new pronouncement that the Bible prohibits women from being pastors of local churches.[25]

Initial reactions to the *2000 BF&M* revision focused on one sentence in Article VI. The Church: "While both men and women are gifted for service in the church, the office of pastor is limited to men as qualified by Scripture."[26] This latest revision of the Baptist confessional statements moves from putting women in their place in the home to assigning females their place in the church. Criticism of this position was immediate, centering on two key factors: biblical interpretation and local church autonomy. Strong reactions appeared in speeches, sermons, articles, editorials, and state convention resolutions. Robert Parham, director of the Baptist Center for Ethics in Nashville, said the new document "pulls up a drawbridge into the 21st century and padlocks Southern Baptists into a 19th century cultural castle." Daniel Vestal, coordinator of the moderate Cooperative Baptist Fellowship, told the New York Times the proposed revision "is based on a bad interpretation of Scripture, an insensitivity to the Holy Spirit and an unwillingness to see what God is doing in the world today."[27]

Committee members defended their prohibition of women as pastors. Al Mohler declared the statement is "not culturally driven" but "a matter of biblical conviction." James Merritt, who ran unopposed as SBC President in 2000, asserted the practice of ordaining women is "unbiblical." Paige Patterson added, "Our positions are not going to be dictated by culture. They're going to be dictated by Scripture."[28]

It is most interesting that committee members brought up the issue of culture—actually, that issue is one of the most serious weaknesses of the SBC framers' position on female roles. Historically, Southern Baptists often have been guilty of reflecting culture more than challenging it. On the issue of race, for over a century Southern Baptists used the Bible to defend slavery and the practice of keeping African Americans in "their place." Both of us were seminary students in the 1960s, and we well remember how Scripture was misused to prove racial inequality and support racial discrimination.

These same arguments, and often the same Scriptures, are now used to support female inequality and discrimination. To their credit, most of the SBC leaders have finally got it right on the race question, but they fail to see the connection with female equality. In supporting their position, the defenders of the traditional view of women's roles play "Bible Poker," flinging down on the table proof-text Scriptures. Traditionalists fear to admit that the Bible must be interpreted in the cultural context in which the Word of God was first delivered, which is a basic hermeneutical principle.[29]

As we examine carefully these recent SBC pronouncements about women, we are forced to conclude that all three are flawed biblically, theologically, and procedurally. Biblically, the framers of these documents have used the Bible selectively, as well as used a method of interpretation that every first-year seminary student is warned to avoid. To quote proof-texts out of context, to add non-biblical words like "graciously," and to attach questionable commentary raises basic hermeneutical suspicions. Theologically, the group proposes a false hierarchical view of marriage and male authority based on the patriarchal idea that men answer to God and women answer to men.

The procedural flaws may not be as obvious. To understand who was chosen to serve on these key committees and how they functioned, especially in comparison to similar committees in the past, is a commentary on power politics in religion. In 1963 there were twenty-four representative people on the *BF&M* committee, one from each state convention, who sought feedback and information from a wide spectrum of resources. Compare this to the seven members in 1998 (one SBC executive, two state convention executives, two wives of seminary presidents, and two pastors) and the thirteen men and two women appointed to the *2000 BF&M* committee. All were known for their extreme right position on most issues, and they deliberately worked in secret until just before the convention.

Another procedural concern has emerged in relation to the application of this document. The preamble to *2000 BF&M* clearly states that "we do not regard them as complete statements of our faith, having any quality of finality or infallibility" and that the statements "are not to be used to hamper freedom of thought or investigation in other realms of life."[30] Yet, despite the traditional Baptist aversion to creeds at every level—national, state, associational, and church—Baptists are now being required to endorse this statement or face ostracism, isolation, or downright expulsion! Local church autonomy and the priesthood of every believer, long-cherished doctrines among Baptists, are now being threatened by this push for SBC-style uniformity, which resembles a hierarchical form of church government that Baptists in America have opposed since the days of Roger Williams, John Leland, and Isaac Backus.

Even though *2000 BF&M* only forbids women to serve as pastors, the practical fallout has been disastrous. SBC seminaries, mission agencies, state offices, and churches have regressed in their recognition and use of women. In the seminary where I taught (along with the other SBC seminaries), women can be considered to teach only "safe subjects" such as music, children and youth work, social work, and religious education. At the Baptist school from which I graduated in 1957, a wonderful female Old Testament professor taught some of our most admired ultra-conservative pastors. No one complained. Today that same school will not consider any woman to teach as a Bible professor.

Just before this chapter was sent to the publisher, I received an email from my former Teaching Assistant/Grader, who this year received her Ph.D. in New Testament. Although she and one other were the first women to receive a doctorate in New Testament from the seminary in New Orleans, that fact was not announced. To add insult to injury, both of them were presented differently than were the male graduates, treated in a way that was condescending and demeaning at the graduation ceremonies.[31]

In many SBC churches women cannot teach men or boys, cannot chair a mixed-gender committee, cannot stand behind the pulpit, cannot lead music—where will this craziness end? This is the fallout from these formal declarations about the place of women in our homes and churches.

As we implied at the beginning, this controversy has a personal side for us. In 1998 as we were preparing for our second sabbatical study, the new seminary president startled Joe with the words, "Have you thought about early retirement?" After a year of sabbatical study our plan was to return to teach for another five to ten years. "You are not being forced to retire," said the president, "but I urge you to consider this window of opportunity." Since 1985, Joe had been the only teacher of Christian ethics at the New Orleans seminary. In many ways he had brought renown to the school, including the publishing of two textbooks widely used.[32] He could not understand the offer until he was told by a reliable source, "Your position on women as outlined in your new textbook could cause problems with our trustees. Our new president will not be able to protect you." A few months later, the SBC approved the *1998 Family Amendment*, which the president's sister helped to frame. And the president himself would soon be on the 2000 committee, even though he later told Joe that he was no theologian and asked his brother-in-law not to appoint him. If we returned to the seminary, our days were numbered. An agreement was reached whereby we did not return.

Helping to put women in their place is a deep conviction we both treasure, as do many others who, like us, consider integrity more valuable than job security. A new advertising logo at CBE says it best: "Put Women in Their Place—Beside Men!" ✝

NOTES

[1] Although there are numerous types of Baptists all holding various views about women, the editors have chosen to use "Baptists" and "Southern Baptists" as synonymous terms, as the debate over female equality has become a major divisive issue in the largest Protestant denomination in America.

[2] The *Baptist Faith and Message 2000* document, written by a committee of which the professor's husband, the president of the seminary, was a member.

[3] See "Woman Overboard" by Penny Glaesman in *Mutuality* (Fall 2001): 16, published by Christians for Biblical Equality, 122 West Franklin Ave., Suite 218, Minneapolis, MN 55404.

[4] Readers who wish to understand the SBC controversy should read Grady C. Cothan, *What Happened to the Southern Baptist Convention* (Macon GA: Smyth & Helwys, 1993) or Fisher Humphreys, *The Way We Were* (Macon GA: Smyth & Helwys, 2002). For the ultra-conservative viewpoint, see Paul Pressler, *A Hill on Which to Die: One Southern Baptist's Journey* (Nashville: Broadman & Holman, 1999).

[5] Russell H. Dilday, "An Analysis of The Baptist Faith and Message 2000," *Christian Ethics Today* 40 (June 2002): 4. This article may be accessed from <www.ChristianEthicsToday.com>.

[6] For a full discussion of the issue of human equality and gender, see Joe E. Trull, *Walking in the Way: An Introduction to Christian Ethics* (Nashville: Broadman & Holman, 1993), 189-211.

[7] A full statement of the organization's beliefs and mission, as well as the endorsement of over 100 leading evangelicals, may be found at their website: <cbe@cbeinternational.org> or by writing to them at 122 W. Franklin Ave., Suite 218, Minneapolis, MN 55404.

[8] Advertisement in *Christianity Today*, 13 January 1989, 40-41, whose address is P.O. Box 1173, Wheaton, IL 60187.

[9] Ibid.

[10] John Piper and Wayne Grudem, eds., *Recovering Biblical Manhood and Womanhood* (Wheaton: Crossway Books, 1991). Only 3 of the 26 chapters, 25 of the 566 pages, are written by women.

[11] See Agnieszka Tennant, "Nuptial Agreements," *Christianity Today*, 11 March 2002, 58-65, for a good summary of the present debate between evangelicals on the issue of gender roles.

[12] Margaret A. Farley, "Feminist Ethics," *The Westminster Dictionary of Christian Ethics*, ed. James F. Childress (Philadelphia: The Westminster Press, 1986), 199-200.

[13] See Elizabeth Achtemeier's "Why God Is Not Mother," *Christianity Today*, 16 August 1993, 16-23.

[14] Tony W. Cartledge, "Positive Signs or Posturing" in the *Biblical Recorder*, 12 July 2002.

[15] Juliette Mather, "Women, Convention Privileges of," *Encyclopedia of Southern Baptists* (Nashville: Broadman Press, 1958), 2:1543.

[16] Ibid., 1544.

[17] Catherine Allen, "Women's Movements and Southern Baptists," *Encyclopedia of Southern Baptists* (1984), 4:2561.

[18] Cothan, *What Happened to the Southern Baptist Convention*, 145.

[19] See *Annual of the Southern Baptist Convention 1984*.

[20] Betty McGary Pearce, "A History of Women in Ministry, SBC," *Folio*, Summer 1985, 9-10.

[21] Dr. Sarah Frances Anders, who has been keeping data on the number of ordained SBC women since the ordination of Addie Davis in 1964, confirms 1788 in 2002, but she estimates the number to be over 1900 including 378 Chaplains; 224 Pastors, Associate, and Co-Pastors; 163 Staff Members; 28 Professors; 25 Other Denominations; 22 Retired; 9 Missionaries; 6 Students; 3 Deceased; and 951 Other (Secular, Wives, etc.). BWIM Board Members believe the number is over 2000.

[22] The full text may be found in the *Baptist Message*, 25 June 1998, 6-7, or in the *Annual of the Southern Baptist Convention 1998*.

[23] Rebecca Merrill Groothuis, "Logical and Theological Problems with Gender Hierarchy" in *Pricilla Papers,* Spring 2000, 3-5. Also worth reading are her two classic books: *Women Caught in the Conflict: The Culture War Between Traditionalism and Feminism* (Grand Rapids: Baker Book House, 1994) and *Good News for Women: A Biblical Picture of Gender Equality* (Baker Book House, 1997).

[24] "Patterson's Election Seals Conservative Control," *Christianity Today*, 13 July 1998, 21.

[25] Dilday, "An Analysis of The Baptist Faith and Message 2000," 4-11.

[26] *The Baptist Faith and Message,* 13, published by LifeWay Christian Resources of the SBC, Nashville TN.

[27] Bob Allen, "Reaction to proposed statement focuses on women's ordination," ABP News, 23 May 2000, vol. 00-45.

[28] Ibid.

[29] Conservative scholars Gordon Fee and Douglass Stuart explain this as "The Problem of Cultural Relativity" (*How to Read the Bible for All Its Worth* [Grand Rapids: Zondervan, 1982], 65-71).

[30] *The Baptist Faith and Message 2000*, 5.

[31] In her words, after the hooding of the graduate, "While the person walks down the steps he is introduced as Dr. So and So who currently is [place of service]. I said 'he' on purpose because this was only done for the men. It was a perfect way once again to humiliate us women. You see women cannot teach in biblical studies or theology. In fact, women cannot even teach Greek . . . . When I was asked what I was currently doing, I said I was nine months pregnant and about to go into labor. So while the men walked down and were presented as Drs., neither woman was presented as Dr." For years these talented women have been committed to missionary service; presently they are seeking appointment by American Baptists because of SBC restrictions on women.

[32] *Walking in the Way: An Introduction to Christian Ethics* (1997) and *Ministerial Ethics* (co-author James Carter, 1993), both published by Broadman & Holman.

CHAPTER ONE

Women and the Southern Baptist Convention

William E. Hull

This article was prompted by two converging emphases. First, media reports have focused on actions taken at meetings of the Southern Baptist Convention (SBC) declaring "the office of pastor is limited to men." This follows a 1998 action directing the wife "to submit herself graciously to the servant leadership of her husband." Second, the annual observances of Mother's Day and Father's Day invite us to reflect on the role of men and women in relation to each other both in the family and in the church. Since the SBC has lifted the model of male headship and female subordination to the level of a core belief in its officially sanctioned statement of "The Baptist Faith and Message" (*BF&M*), it behooves us to consider carefully what this development may mean for our congregation as a cooperating church.

I can already anticipate your negative reaction to a consideration of this agenda. Many in the Baptist pews are tired of hearing about another outbreak of that seemingly endless struggle called the SBC Controversy, which they interpret primarily as a preacher fight for control and power. Many Baptists are either embarrassed or angry over what has happened and would prefer to hear nothing more in the hope that it will somehow go away. In any case, just as Roman Catholic laity are not willing to let the hierarchy in Rome tell them whether to practice birth control, so Baptist laity are not about to let the few thousand messengers at a Southern Baptist Convention meeting determine how they relate to members of the opposite sex. The prevailing response thus far seems to be either to complain about, or to joke about, this action and then to hide behind the cherished doctrine of congregational autonomy. I am not convinced that this dismissive attitude represents an adequate response to what the SBC has done.

THE IMPLICATIONS OF THE SBC ACTION

First we need to understand that Baptists have long been cautious about adopting any confession of faith at all, since such statements carry the danger of creedalism against which we reacted strongly from the very beginning of our movement nearly 400 years ago. The SBC had no such statement from its founding in 1845 until 1925 when a bitter controversy over evolution prompted the first such effort. This document served unchanged until 1963 when another bitter controversy over the interpretation of Genesis triggered its revision. From 1845 to 1998, during the first 153 years of its existence, the SBC managed to need only two statements of faith, each prompted by a severe internal crisis. But now, in just the last two years, we have had two more revisions at a time when the current leadership of the Convention is claiming that things could not be going better.

The mystery of why the SBC needs this sudden rash of revisions deepens when we consider that both changes comment on the role of women in relation to men, first in the family (1998) and then in the church (2000). Not a word on this subject appeared in either of our previous statements of 1925 and 1963 or in any other declarations used earlier by Baptists, such as the New Hampshire Confession of 1853. Nor was this matter addressed in any of the classic creeds of Christendom, such as those of Nicea (324) and Chalcedon (451), which have guided the church for almost 2000 years. Here we have a daring new departure in the construction and content of a confession of faith, ironically being pushed by those who like to style themselves as "conservative"!

The plot thickens when we realize that these novel amendments so recently enacted have long been controversial and even divisive within our Baptist fellowship. Indeed, the framers of these additions, which included two seminary presidents, were well aware that their key contentions regarding the place of women in the Christian faith are vigorously contested, not just by so-called "moderates," but by those of their own theological persuasion called "inerrantists."[1] In cases of deep division within the Baptist ranks, the standard practice has long been to exclude such debated points from a statement of faith. For example, we have never agreed on one view of the millennium and so this doctrine has been omitted from all of our confessions, even though for Dispensationalists a pre-millennial view is crucial to their whole understanding of Scripture. By inserting one hotly debated viewpoint into the latest version of its statement of faith, the SBC has changed the very character of the *BF&M* from a unifying to a polarizing document.

But why should the current SBC leadership want to inject a note of controversy into a document intended to strengthen consensus at a time when even its proponents acknowledge that there is no urgent problem in need of correction? The drafting committee itself released a study which showed that "no more than 35 women are senior pastors in more that 41,000 Southern Baptist churches nationwide,"[2] scarcely a threat to the status quo of male dominance in the ministry. But while practices have hardly begun to change, the underlying attitudes toward gender relations do differ significantly within our Baptist family. An emphasis upon the complete equality of women to exercise their spiritual gifts within both the home and the church is characteristic of such diverse groups as the Cooperative Baptist Fellowship, the Alliance of Baptists, the dozen or so seminaries founded recently under Baptist sponsorship, most of the fifty-plus Baptist colleges and universities, Smyth and Helwys Publishers, Woman's Missionary Union national organization and many of its state organizations, the Baptist Joint Committee, and, of course, Baptist Women in Ministry.

It is in an effort to reject this viewpoint, to stifle this dissent, to eliminate these differences that the additions regarding women have been made to the *BF&M*. We may assume that these changes reflect the sincere faith of their supporters but, in choosing this means to express their faith, the architects of the *2000 BF&M* made its adoption an exercise in the politics of exclusion. Rather than both sides studying the issue together and seeking to resolve our differences by patient investigation and friendly dialogue, a decision was made to cut off discussion and settle the matter decisively, not by deeper study of the biblical evidence or by weighing the merits of divergent viewpoints, but by majority vote of assembled messengers. If that sounds at first like the democratic thing to do, I would observe that, if Baptists could have handled the abolition question that way, we would still have slaves in the South! The plain fact is that equal rights are seldom if ever extended to an excluded group until after they have first been denied again and again by an overwhelming majority of those in power wishing to maintain the status quo.

Faced with the finality of the SBC action and the futility of trying to overturn it, some might be tempted to say, "Let's just ignore what they did and plot our own course for the future." The freedom to do that very thing is a precious heritage, which continues to be affirmed in the *2000 BF&M*

where the church is defined as "an autonomous local congregation . . . [which] operates under the Lordship of Christ through democratic processes."[3] But the solution is not that simple because the SBC influences the life of its member churches in a number of direct and inescapable ways. Let me offer but three illustrations of how the SBC position on women will impact Baptist congregations in the days ahead.

1. Congregations could decide to stay with the *1963 BF&M*, but every professional employee of SBC agencies are being required to subscribe to the *2000 BF&M* as a condition of employment. This means that pastors or ministerial staff who come to churches from SBC seminaries will have been taught by faculty unanimously in support of these changes, that missionaries who visit to commend the Lottie Moon and Annie Armstrong offerings will henceforth be expected to endorse these changes, that Sunday school literature ordered from LifeWay Resources will be prepared by writers who accept these changes. There are upward of 15,000 employees in SBC agencies whose job it is to support and extend the work of 40,000-plus Baptist churches. Now that they have gotten their marching orders, we should not be surprised if changes to the *BF&M* continue to become a pervasive influence in much of Baptist life.

2. In Baptist polity, not only are local churches autonomous but regional, state, national, and international bodies are autonomous as well, which means that the SBC has no authority to superimpose its confessional views at other levels of our denominational life. This might encourage those who are unhappy with the SBC action to channel their cooperative efforts through alternate agencies, like state or local Baptist agencies which have not adopted the SBC position on women.[4] But pressure will be applied on these bodies by SBC supporters to adopt the *2000 BF&M*, at least in principle, partly because the SBC is so much larger than any of these other bodies and also because they are all closely linked to the SBC through complex funding mechanisms. Even if such pressures are resisted, the effort itself will be disruptive, introducing needless dissension into our ranks, distracting us from our central mission, and giving the media another field day to ridicule the whole controversy.

3. Perhaps the hardest problem for those who would advocate a strategy of avoidance is the fact that many local Baptist churches have long contributed

generously through the Cooperative Program to the support of every SBC agency. But because some of these churches, like my own Baptist church in Birmingham, have ordained women to the ministry and to the diaconate, practices that are not expressly forbidden by the *2000 BF&M*, none of their members are being considered for positions of service on the board of any SBC agency. Solely on the basis of granting to women an equal rather than a subordinate role in the life of their church, they are denied any voice in the policy-making councils of those agencies that have been prime beneficiaries of their missions giving for decades. My own church, Mountain Brook, probably has more members than any other church in Alabama with the requisite experience to oversee the large business operations of SBC agencies, as has long been demonstrated by their service on the Samford Board of Trustees, yet not only are we boycotted from having any representation but so is every other church that shares our attitude toward women in church leadership.

Therefore, if we cannot simply ignore this issue because of our deep denominational ties, then what should we do about it? I believe that we could make any one of at least three mistakes in formulating a strategy for responding to this problem.

1. We could wait patiently for the government to solve our problem. After all, time is on our side. Women are entering fully into all of the other major professions, such as law, medicine, and education. They now sit on the Supreme Court, are members of Congress, and aggressively campaign for the Presidency in both parties. In case you missed it, equal opportunity for women is now the law of the land, making discrimination by reason of gender illegal. Our seminaries are sending out a stream of talented women who have earned both standard and advanced degrees in pastoral ministry (M.Div., D.Min). Churches will find it increasingly risky to ignore candidates for ministry positions simply because they are female, especially if they are the most highly qualified applicants. My guess is that the courts will be slow to enforce equal opportunity rights for women seeking pastoral employment. Rather, the greater pressure will come from public outrage, as when George W. Bush's campaign visit to Bob Jones University resulted in a firestorm of criticism that prompted the institution to rescind its discrimination policy against interracial dating that the government had long sought to overturn by revoking its tax-exempt status.

2. Men could punt and wait for women to solve the problem that we created. After all, women constitute a clear majority of church members. Moreover, they are rapidly gaining leadership skills and financial clout in the workplace. At least some of them have learned hard-nosed negotiating skills from the feminist movement that they could adapt to the Byzantine world of denominational politics. But I do not look for women to unite in reversing the SBC action for a seldom-recognized reason. Many women are so afraid that their men will neglect family responsibilities—either because of intense business pressures to succeed, or because of addiction to football and fishing, or because our sexually permissive culture encourages them to dump the wife for a plaything half her age—that they will gladly let them be "head" and submit to them "graciously" if only this will apply enough religious pressure to keep them faithful and encourage them to help raise the kids.

3. We could complain about the *2000 BF&M* and criticize those who engineered its changes in the hope that if we protest the problem long enough it might be corrected by a groundswell of opposition. There are two defects in this strategy. First, such constant carping makes us crabby, negative, and defensive. Nobody is attracted to a movement that is forever whining about what somebody else did. Second, we are not about to overturn this change by political action, whether it is negative or positive. Of the 11,800 messengers gathered in Orlando in 2000, "only a few dozen cast dissenting votes."[5] The supporters of the new orthodoxy are solidly united and well disciplined, convinced that they are courageously following the literal dictates of Scripture while their detractors are bending to the trendy winds of modern culture. Of course, that is exactly what Southern preachers said 150 years ago when defending slavery, but all such arguments fall on deaf ears because the other side is not paying any attention to us. By their own admission, they would be happy if churches like ours would just leave the SBC so that they would no longer have to contend with our contrarian witness. There can be little doubt that the recent revisions of the *BF&M* were undertaken partly in an effort to encourage such a separation.

THE IMPERATIVES OF THE BIBLICAL WITNESS[6]

In a situation such as this, we cannot take refuge in congregational autonomy, in Baptist tradition, or in political superiority. Therefore we are driven of necessity to state everything on our best understanding of the will of God as revealed in Holy Scripture. Fortunately, this is the one point on which all sides agree. As Gardendale pastor Steve Gaines is reported to have said, "The burden of proof is on them to find it [i.e., gender equality that would permit women pastors] in the Scripture,"[7] a challenge we should gladly accept. If we can hammer out a clearer, wiser interpretation of the Bible than those who endorsed the views now found in the *2000 BF&M*, those scriptural convictions will trump a majority vote every time. Instead of assuming that the issue is now settled, let us diligently search the word and boldly proclaim the fullness of its truth in the confidence that God will vindicate our efforts in his own good time, just as he did for the opponents of slavery who urged its abolition against an overwhelming majority.

The Bible does not paint a pretty picture of the place woman occupied in the ancient world. We need not be squeamish, however, about acknowledging her low estate even within Scripture, such as concubinage and polygamy. The issue for us is not how much progress was actually achieved during the millennium covered by biblical literature, but whether God chose that often deplorable situation in which to disclose his ultimate intention for woman. In the Bible we find actual rather than ideal social conditions, in some respects better but in other respects worse than those obtained elsewhere. What this means is that God did not necessarily pick out the most advanced society in which to work, but that he was willing to deal with a sometimes progressive and a sometimes regressive situation as he found it. Such a realization offers the hope that our wayward world may yet have a chance for divine help even in those cultures where women are still brutally exploited.

How may we determine the distinctive contours of biblical faith and the center around which that faith coheres? The focal point is clearly Christ and all that he means for the life of humanity. Jesus himself recognized that without a christocentric hermeneutic the unity of Scripture would be destroyed (Matt 5:17-18). But the reality of Christ may be fully understood only if set in the context of a redemptive drama stretching from the creation to the consummation. These three realities, taken together, are constitutive for biblical faith because, in them as nowhere else, divine truth from beyond history most clearly impinges upon the whole of God's redemptive history. It is from this threefold perspective that woman may be viewed both in the light of the painful realities of this world and in the light of the perfected realities of the world to come.

Woman and Creation. The oldest and in many ways the most comprehensive biblical witness to the place of woman as defined by creation is found in

7

Genesis 2:4b-25. There we meet the male in his solitude as an incomplete creation: it was *"not good* that he should be alone" (2:18a, my italics). When no other living creature could be found to fill that void (2:19-20), God fashioned woman to be a companion "corresponding" to him (literally: "a helper according to what is in front of him"; that is, a kind of mirror image of his humanity). When man was presented with his "opposite number," he immediately rejoiced to discover that in her he now had both otherness (i.e., community) and sameness (i.e., "bone of my bones and flesh of my flesh," 2:23), a relationship he could never sustain with the animals. So necessary was each to the other that their attachment was to transcend every other loyalty, even the blood tie between parent and child (2:24). Just as a piece of paper, by its nature, has two sides, so humanity, by its created nature, has two sexes. Neither the male nor the female alone, but only the two of them together as "one flesh," constitute and complete what it means generically to be human.

Because this account depicts woman as having been created *after* man, *from* man, and *for* man, some have seen in its concept of complementary companionship a theology of female subordination of which there is no hint in the text. Any doubt is dispelled by the creation account given pride of place in Genesis 1:26-31. There, "God created man in his own image," creating "male and female" concurrently (1:27). Gender differentiation was inherent in God's design for humanity from the outset: the female was not an accident, an afterthought, or an expedient. A paradoxical singularity and plurality of being ("God created *him*; male and female created he *them*," 1:27, my italics) corresponded to or "imaged" a similar reciprocity in God's being ("Let *us* make man . . . *he* created him/them," 1:26-27, my italics). We, like God, were meant to be a fellowship within ourselves though, unlike God, our internal duality is defined by gender.

But that essential partnership of male and female was shattered by the impulse of the two genders to achieve their destiny separately (Gen 3). At first there was no shame in their nakedness (2:25) because they saw each other in their solidarity, but, once the serpent had exploited their pride to drive the wedge of alienation, they began to see each other in terms of their differences (3:11-13) and so covered their nakedness (3:7). As punishment for her effort to redefine the ultimate meaning of life in terms of what she could get rather than what she could give, woman exchanged a possible paradise for the pain of childbirth, the burdens of raising a large family, and the domination of her husband (3:16).

So much has been made of these afflictions imposed on woman that they deserve further comment, especially the final one on subjection to the husband ("he shall rule over you"). Note the following: (a) The husband's rule was not arbitrarily imposed like that of a conquering despot but functioned in the context of her continuing "desire" for him (3:16b). (b) The punishment was not sexually discriminatory since man was given an equal share of problems (3:17-19). Just as fertility for the woman was found in the womb where she would toil in pain to produce, so fertility for the man was found in the soil where he likewise would toil "in the sweat of his face" to produce. (c) The terms of the sentence described conditions as they actually existed for both women and men in the ancient world; that is, the story helped to account for the darker side of human existence by attributing it to judgment for sin. The point cannot be stressed too strongly that these consequences of human folly were not divine ordinances decreed for all time; rather, "these are evils which the author feels to be contrary to the ideal of human nature, and to the intention of a good God."[8]

This insight is crucial to an interpretation of the place of woman in the biblical doctrine of creation. The whole structure of the account in 2:4b–3:24 was designed to magnify the contrast between the ideal intention for woman created by God (2:18-25) and the tragic alternative that she and her mate created for themselves by flaunting the divine order. But this means, further, that it was precisely her sexual plight—because it rooted in sin rather than in God—that the whole history of salvation is working to redeem. The Bible never understood divine punishment as an eternal curse. Rather, tragedies permitted by God as the price of humanity's freedom to fail were transformed by him at infinite cost as a result of the divine determination to succeed. Male dominance and female subjection were very real. They belonged to the Old Age of fallen humanity that had not yet passed away. But they did not belong to God's good creation. They were not a part of the way things were meant to be.

Jesus, of course, was the supreme interpreter of creation theology within the Bible (Matt 19:3-9/Mark 10:2-12). In response to a question regarding the rights of a man to divorce his wife, he identified the Mosaic legislation of Deuteronomy 24:1-4 as an effort to deal with "hardness of heart" but, over against that, set the "beginning of creation" (Mark 10:6) when "it was not so" (Matt 19:8). It is significant that Jesus attributed to sin the male dominance seen so clearly in the unfair divorce laws of his day. By contrast, he based his positive understanding of gender differences on a fusion of the key elements in

Genesis 1:27 and 2:24, thereby acknowledging both the unity and the primacy of these passages. For him, God had "joined together" two equal partners as "one," thereby ruling out not only the male prerogative of divorce but any other form of unfaithfulness by either partner which would weaken the marriage bond (Mark 10:11-12).

Unlike Jesus, Paul did have occasion to refer to the subordination of woman rooted in Genesis 3:16 (cf. 1 Cor 11:3-9; 14:34; Eph 5:22-24; 1 Tim 2:11-15). In so doing, however, he was careful to maintain the unity and equality of the sexes in the creative purpose of God (1 Cor 11:11-12; Eph 5:28-33; and, by implication, 1 Cor 6:16). The clue to this apparent dichotomy of status is found in Paul's understanding of God's unfolding salvation. As Romans 5–8 makes clear, he saw Christians living where the Old Age and the New Age impinged or "overlapped" (1 Cor 10–11). Insofar as they still lived "in the world," in a fallen creation subjected to futility and bondage (Rom 8:20-21), male dominance and female subjection were ever-present realities that could not be ignored lest social chaos erupt and Christianity be branded as a libertine escapist movement. But insofar as they now lived "in the Lord," in a creation destined to "obtain the glorious liberty" that already belonged to the children of God (Rom 8:21), these cultural restrictions were already transcended. In the eyes of the world, women at worship could be completely misunderstood if they did not keep silent (1 Cor 14:34; 1 Tim 2:11), whereas in the eyes of faith these same women were free to pray and prophesy or even to teach (1 Cor 11:5; Titus 2:3).

Woman and Christ. For the Bible, the meaning of the Christ was uniquely incarnated in the historical ministry of Jesus. It is striking that his message nowhere included references to circumcision, that distinctively male rite of initiation from which Jewish women and female proselytes were excluded. In place of this ancient practice that had assumed such importance in first century Judaism (Eph 2:11), Jesus focused on faith as the basis of one's standing before God. This immediately put women, as well as foreigners, on equal footing with Jewish males (Mark 5:34; Matt 8:10). Moreover, he demanded that women make their own personal commitment to him even if it shattered the solidarity of the family (Matt 10:34-36; Luke 12:51-53). In response, women formed a special band that accompanied him from Galilee, several of whom were so prominent that their names have become a part of the gospel record (Luke 8:2-3). "The fact that women followed Jesus is without precedent in contemporary Judaism."[9]

Examples might be multiplied of the ways in which women became an integral part of Jesus' ministry. In contrast to Jewish parallels, both Jesus' parables and his miracles often dealt tenderly with women. He talked to them in public (John 4:27) and made friends of them in the home (Luke 10:38-42). No wonder they were the last at the cross in courage (Matt 27:55-56), the first at the tomb in compassion (Mark 16:1). The important point to grasp here is the theological reality underlying this remarkable pattern. Albrecht Oepke provides a clue: "Jesus is not the radical reformer who proclaims laws and seeks to enforce a transformation of relationships. He is the Savior who gives Himself especially to the lowly and oppressed and calls all without distinction to the freedom of the Kingdom of God."[10]

That is why the Apostle Paul could affirm, in the clearest expression of his christocentric faith: "there is no 'male and female'; for you are all one in Christ Jesus" (Gal 3:28). Viewed historically, behind that claim lay the important role of women in the founding of the church (Acts 1:14; 2:17; 12:12), in the spread of the missionary movement (Acts 16:13-15; 17:4, 12, 34; 18:18, 26), and in positions of leadership and service (Rom 16:1, 3, 6, 12, 15). But viewed theologically, here is not merely the claim that in Christ the "male and female" duality of creation has been redeemed from its corruption by sin, but also that in the life of the Body of Christ (3:27) it has actually been transcended. The children of God who live by a faith (3:26) expressed in baptism (3:27a) have thereby been "clothed" with a Christ-identity (3:27b) that supersedes racial, social, and sexual identities.

Woman and the Consummation. Both Jewish and Christian thought distinguished between the Messianic Age on earth and the Age to Come in the world beyond. The basic difference was that, for Judaism, these two epochs lay beyond the final period of human history and so were sharply discontinuous with the old dispensation, whereas, for Christianity, Jesus brought the Messianic Age into the midst of history, thereby fulfilling the Old Age and foreshadowing the Age to Come at the end of history. Let us see how this distinctive outlook affected the biblical theology of woman.

During the ministry of Jesus, the Sadducees sought to snare him with a particularly offensive illustration of levirate marriage to seven successive brothers (Matt 22:23-33/Mark 12:18-27/Luke 20:27-40) on which basis they asked, "In the resurrection whose wife will she be?" (Mark 12:23), hoping thereby to justify their rejection of the future life by ridiculing its premises. In his response, "when they rise from the dead they neither marry nor are given in marriage, but are like angels in heaven" (Mark 12:25), Jesus exposed a basic fallacy: his opponents had not reckoned with "the power of God" to fashion an order so completely different from earth that it need not perpetuate any of its ambiguities. Since the angels were in the heavenly court prior to creation, they must be non-fleshly creatures and therefore without gender. When the husbands and wives of earth exchange their physical bodies for spiritual bodies (1 Cor 15:44), they obviously leave the earthly institution of marriage behind. Oepke traces the implications of this vision for Jesus' hearers: "In holding out the prospect of sexless being like that of the angels in the consummated kingdom of God, He indirectly lifts from woman the curse of her sex and sets her at the side of man as equally a child of God."[11]

Paul entertained a similar view that helps to explain one of the most puzzling passages in his epistles: "The appointed time has grown very short; from now on, let those who have wives live as though they had none . . . . For the form of this world is passing away" (1 Cor 7:29-31). The Apostle was aware that, sooner than most realize, the whole order to which marriage belongs would terminate—whether at the end of world history through the return of Christ or at the end of each individual's personal history through death—and therefore now was the time to prepare for that impending heavenly existence. This could be done neither by divorce (7:27) nor by separation or sexual restraint (7:3-5), but by practicing an "undivided devotion to the Lord" (7:35). The intensity of Paul's commitment to the world beyond was remarkable indeed: so clearly did the Age to Come loom on his spiritual horizon that he was ready for it to reshape the most intimate relationships of earthly life.

When we put all of the relevant passages together they coalesce into a coherent perspective that sets human sexuality into a "saving history" framework. Both Jesus and Paul recognized three distinct "ages" or stages in the relationship of male and female: (1) The Old Age, in which "hardness of heart" led to male dominance, female subjection, unfaithfulness, and exploitation; (2) The Messianic Age, in which Christ makes possible a realization of the original intention for man and woman in the created order, namely an equality of reciprocal loyalty, fidelity, and support; and (3) The Age to Come, in which our earthly relationships will be transcended and our unity-in-reciprocity will be fulfilled, not by oneness with opposite sex, but by a perfect oneness with God-in-Christ.

This biblical perspective on woman may be applied most relevantly in two respects. Historically, we may ask where the church in our generation wishes to be located on this salvation timetable. Shall we revert once more to the Old Age, as if woman had not been punished enough, and seek new ways to keep her in subjection? Or shall we take seriously the fact that Christ has come and liberated both male and female from their age-long strife to new possibilities of mutual respect and caring? Indeed, dare we push our spirits to the boundary where time itself shall be no more in order to go beyond a careful equality and mutuality of the sexes to a realm of pure spiritual adventure in Christ where gender matters not at all? These same questions may also be asked personally as I decide just how far I am willing to recapitulate in my own experience the age-long quest to regain Paradise Lost and see woman as she was meant to be, the indispensable "otherness" without whom my humanity is incomplete, and by truly finding her to discover beyond us both that essential humanity which lives both now and forevermore with "undivided devotion to the Lord."

GENDER EQUALITY IN THE LIFE OF THE CHURCH

The biblical convictions we have just surveyed can be as much of a liberating force in the twenty-first-century church as they were in the first century church. All over the world, Christians are finding new vitality by offering unlimited spiritual fulfillment to both halves of the human race. Interestingly enough, much of this activity is found on the conservative side of the theological spectrum where the SBC claims to be positioning itself. Gary Parker has cited three examples: (1) Promise Keepers has opened its clergy meetings to women because, as founder Bill McCartney explained, "We have learned that thirteen percent of our churches are pastored by ladies." (2) Willow Creek Church, known internationally for its "seeker services," does not, according to pastor Bill Hybels, "restrict any office or position in the church on the basis of gender." (3) Billy Graham, when asked by David Frost about women's ordination, said, "Women preach all over the world. It doesn't bother me at all from my study of the Scriptures."[12]

At bottom, it really does not matter if we are "for" gender equality in our church unless it makes a difference in the effectiveness with which we minister. Let us prove by the health of our congregation that we can do God's work better when we utilize the contribution of male and female alike without restriction. There is not opportunity here even to list, much less to discuss, the many ways that the life of our congregation can be enriched by encouraging the full participation of women on the same basis as men. Let me select three areas to illustrate how men and women can work together in a partnership of equals as servants of Christ.

The Initiative of God. Baptists have always based the authorization for ministry not on apostolic succession, but on the call of God. Therefore it is only logical that some who support the *2000 BF&M* would claim that God does not call women to be pastors. The theology behind this assumption is not unlike that of an early Christian group called Judaizers who insisted that one must follow their ancient traditions—that is, embrace circumcision, Sabbath observance, and temple sacrifice—in order to become a Christian. But God kept running ahead of this restrictive theology and saving Gentiles *before* they embraced these Jewish practices. When, for example, Peter was criticized for baptizing the uncircumcised Cornelius (Acts 10:1-48), his defense was that God had validated the centurion's conversion by filling him with the Holy Spirit quite apart from meeting any of the conditions imposed by the Judaizers (Acts 11:1-18).

Note carefully the key principle that Peter learned from this experience: "If then God gave the same gift to them as he gave to us when we believed in the Lord Jesus Christ, who was I that I could withstand God?" (Acts 11:17). Here is a situation in which theology was being challenged to catch up with experience. For centuries, pious Jews had believed that Scripture was telling them to circumcise every convert, a practice that became urgently important to them in the first century when they felt threatened with extinction through cultural assimilation. But now a new day had dawned when their understanding of what God had *said* was being reinterpreted by what God had actually *done!* This explains why circumcision, a dominant practice throughout the Old Testament, was dropped almost immediately in the New Testament, never again to become a restriction limiting Gentile participation in the Christian movement.

Baptists today face the same situation in regard to women as Peter did in regard to Gentiles. For generations we were rooted in the soil on farms or as laborers and shopkeepers in the cities. In that social system, men did the "public" work while women stayed at home, thus it was only natural for men to exercise leadership in the churches. But now all of that has changed. Most of our Baptist women are in the workplace where equal employment opportunities are taken for granted. Years ago, few women indeed heard God's call to minister, except perhaps in a very different culture on some foreign field. After all, back then they could not even gain admission to an SBC seminary to receive the training needed for such service. Today, when all of the educational opportunities available to men are also open to women, when women are assuming leadership roles in every other vocation, when there is a chronic shortage of qualified male candidates for ministry, is it any wonder that many more women are hearing and heeding God's call to ministry?

Baptists place a high priority on personal religious experience. If a young man steps forward and declares with clarity and conviction that God has called him to the ministry, we are almost certain to ordain him after examination by a council of mature church leaders. How, then, can we do otherwise if a young woman steps forward, if her testimony is radiant with an impelling sense of God's call, if her understanding of Baptist faith and practice is sound and sensible, if she is willing to prove the sincerity of her dedication through years of sacrificial preparation, if her abilities are equal or superior to those of many male ministers? With Peter we must ask, "Who are we to hinder the freedom of God to call whom he will?" Dare we limit his grace by our inherited traditions? Let us learn to rejoice rather than to resist when God is ready to do a new thing in our midst.

A Representative Ministry. Turning now from the divine to the human side of the equation, Baptists began as a lay movement and that of necessity because ordination was controlled by the state church. For this reason we emphasize the priesthood of every believer rather than viewing the ministry as some "official" group with a special status denied to other members. We take seriously the promise of Acts 2:17-18 that God's Spirit is now available to all, whether they be male or female, young or old, master or servant. It is in the power of the Spirit that every Christian ministers, whether it be to prophesy, to see visions, or to dream dreams. As the entire Book of Acts makes clear, it is not by ordination but by spiritual empowerment that God's work is done in our world.

Then why do Baptists set apart ministers and deacons by ordination? Clearly they are meant to be leaders who are representative of the entire ministering membership rather that to be what the *2000 BF&M* calls "scriptural officers" of the church. The requirements of the democratic process demand some such arrangement. Obviously a congregation of several thousand members, as was the case from the beginning at Pentecost, cannot conduct its business as a committee of the whole. And so manageable groups, such as the Twelve and the Seven, soon began to function on behalf of the larger body (Acts 6:1-6). In the first century, it was customary for such leadership groups to be exclusively male, since women had virtually no legal rights or public role in society, being cared for by their fathers if single, by their husbands if married, or by their eldest sons if widowed. But it may be noted that female leadership groups did emerge with qualifications comparable to those for bishops and deacons (1 Tim 3:1, 8, 11), possibly to care for the large number of widows who had no immediate family to provide support (1 Tim 5:3-16).

Today, however, the situation is totally different. Not only are women totally enfranchised in society, but many of them function as heads of household. For years the argument was made that women could have influence in a male-led church through their husbands, but this assumption ignores not only the rising number of women who have no husband because they are single, divorced, or widowed, but also those women whose husbands are either not Christian, inactive, or members of another church. Let us be both honest and practical: is there an all-male clergy or diaconate anywhere that can claim to understand and minister to the deepest needs of half or more of the members who are female? Of equal seriousness: what does it say about *all* Christians being a priesthood of believers if there are no women serving as priests in the leadership of the church?

It is neither candid nor consistent for Baptists to give women utterly crucial spiritual responsibilities on the one hand but deny them any status and recognition on the other hand. For example, women have long done more than their share of Bible teaching in the Sunday school, have supported our vast missionary enterprise with almost no help from the men, and have provided virtually all of the leadership for our children and youth during the most formative years of their spiritual development. Functionally, women have been performing many of the most important ministries of the church while, formally, most of the status implied by ordination has been handed out to men. To refuse to correct this imbalance is to perpetuate a "put-down," as if women were somehow inferior to men, and to risk making the "glass ceiling" more cramped in the church than it is in the world.

The Sharing of Gifts. In addition to our emphasis on grace, by which we affirm our willingness to let God give what God will even before we are ready to receive it, Baptists have placed equal stress on the importance of faith, by which we mean that our response is also a crucial component in the divine-human encounter. The sovereign grace of God does not leave us passive but rather frees us to participate gladly in the new thing God is doing. To limit or exclude women from leadership roles in the church or in the home strikes at the heart of this understanding of faith. For we do not decide whether to be male or female; rather, we find ourselves fashioned into one or the other by the reproductive process that God has established for human procreation. The ultimate danger here is to assign a negative value to something that God has done in which we have no choice. Even if we could by scientific means control the gender of our offspring, would we wish to tamper with the approximately equal distribution of males and females?

In place of arbitrary restrictions that would deny women some opportunity for service simply because of their gender, let us magnify the freedom of each person to share fully such spiritual gifts as he or she has been given. Women obviously have a special sensitivity to the needs of other women, particularly in such areas of pregnancy, childcare, and homemaking. What male, whether he be minister or deacon, could possibly be as effective as a female in helping women deal with such intimate crises as infertility, miscarriage, or menopause? Women also need a spiritual sisterhood to see them through such traumas as divorce or widowhood or their own approaching death. But this ministry of women is not limited to other women. Precisely because of their gender, women have their own distinctive expectations of worship, ways of witnessing, theological agenda, ethical concerns, and styles of leadership. Their approaches are not necessarily better than those more typical of men. But they are different because of their rootage in feminine experience and thereby likely to be both relevant to the female half of the church and broadening to the male half of the church.

As we move through the beginning of a new century, Christianity finds itself facing awesome challenges that will require the most courageous and creative leadership of which we are capable. To put it plainly, we are going to need all of the help we can get, whether from clergy or laity. If so, then why respond with one hand tied behind our backs by limiting women with spiritual gifts from serving in any leadership position? If, in Christ and in his body, there really is "neither male nor female" (Gal 3:28), can we not work toward the kind of church in which each of us would just as soon be a man or a woman in terms of the potential that gender offers for spiritual fulfillment?

Such a goal will not be easy to attain simply because Baptists have accepted gender restrictions for centuries. The dilemma is that when we change the way things have been done for hundreds of years our detractors can accuse us of being "liberal" when in actuality we are bring "conservative" to champion realities that have been true for two thousand years. Traditions die hard in the Deep South, none more so than stereotypes regarding the role of women. But remember that women such as Lydia and Priscilla and Phoebe came into their own and furnished crucial leadership to the early church in ways that would have been impossible in the Jewish, Greek, or Roman religions of that day. How ironic! The first century church, despite all of the *limitations* placed on women by its culture, was *ahead* of its time, whereas the twenty-first-century church, despite all of the *opportunities* offered to women by its culture, is in danger of falling *behind* its time. Let us resolve to change provincial Southern traditions at least as much as the early church changed provincial Palestinian traditions in the spirit of the Christ who offers spiritual freedom and equality to all who follow him. ✛

NOTES

[1] See, for example, the statement on "Men, Women and Biblical Equality" issued by Christians for Biblical Equality at <cbe@cbeinternational.org>. A typical book is Stanley J. Grenz with Denise Muir Kjesbo, *Women in the Church: A Biblical Theology of Women in Ministry* (Downers Grove IL: InterVarsity, 1995). Several inerrantists who affirm women in church leadership are listed in Ruth Tucker and Walter Liefeld, *Daughters of the Church: Women and Ministry from New Testament Times to the Present* (Grand Rapids: Zondervan, 1987).

[2] Greg Garrison, *The Birmingham News*, 15 June 2000, 2-A.

[3] Article VI, "The Church."

[4] When the Alabama Baptist State Convention met on 17 November 1998, a resolution was offered "in support of the Southern Baptist Convention's amendment to the Baptist Faith and Message related to the family" that had been adopted by the SBC in Salt Lake City on 9 June 1998. But the State Board of Missions, not the Resolutions Committee, offered instead "A Position Statement on the Family" that omitted entirely the notions of headship and submission in the marital relationship. This splendid statement was duly adopted by the messengers. See the *1998 Annual: Alabama Baptist State Convention,* pp. 71, 105-106. When asked about the omission of SBC language, Convention President Leon Ballard replied, "It was a conscious effort to be sensitive. It's the role of the husband and wife to be individuals. They each bring their individuality to the marriage." Commenting that the word "submit" has been misunderstood and misused, Ballard continued: "I would be careful with that word. Some men have used that against their wives" (Greg Garrison, *The Birmingham News*, 18 November 1998, 1-A).

[5] Greg Garrison, *The Birmingham News*, 15 June 2000, 1-A.

[6] This entire treatment is abridged from a longer study, "Woman in Her Place," *Review & Expositor* 72/1 (Winter 1975): 5-17.

[7] Cited by Greg Garrison, *The Birmingham News*, 18 June 2000, 17-A.

[8] John Skinner, *A Critical and Exegetical Commentary on Genesis* (Edinburgh: T. & T. Clark, 1930), 95 (cf. p. 83).

[9] Werner Foerster, *Palestinian Judaism in New Testament Times* (Edinburgh: Oliver and Boyd, 1964), 127.

[10] Albrecht Oepke, *Theological Dictionary of the New Testament*, vol. 1, ed. Gerhard Kittel (Grand Rapids: William B. Eerdmans, 1964), 784.

[11] Ibid., 785.

[12] Gary E. Parker, "Women in the Pulpit?" *Religious Herald*, 15 June 2000, 8-9. Our Gardendale friend, Steve Gaines, allowed himself to claim that this view of gender equality is "not in the New Testament, it's in feminist thought," but McCartney, Hybels, and Graham are as far from what Gaines means by "feminist thought" as one could imagine (*The Birmingham News*, 18 June 2000, 17-A).

CHAPTER TWO

One Woman's Response to the SBC

By Julie Pennington-Russell

Frederick Buechner writes that when he was a young man one summer day in an elegant house on Long Island, mingling with a number of strangers at a long, elegantly set dinner table, his hostess suddenly asked him a question. She spoke loudly, and at the sound of her question all other conversation stopped and every face turned to hear his answer. "I understand that you are planning to enter the ministry," she said. "Is this your own idea, or have you been poorly advised?"[1]

That particular question has occurred to me once or twice in the twenty years since I entered seminary. I wondered if perhaps I'd been poorly advised when, on the first day of my first seminary preaching class, the professor walked into the room, spied me and one other woman, and then looked over the tops of his glasses and chuckled, saying, "Ah—I see we have two ladies in the class! Well that's marvelous. And you know what I always say, a woman preaching is rather like a dog walking on its hind legs. Neither does it very well, but you're surprised it can be done at all!"[2]

I wondered again if I'd been poorly advised about entering vocational ministry when, for five consecutive years while serving as pastor of Nineteenth Avenue Baptist Church in San Francisco, messengers at the annual California Baptist Convention challenged the seating of our congregation's messengers at the meeting because of my gender. Twice during those five years we were unseated and denied participation.

I wondered yet again if I'd been poorly advised when I was twice invited, then uninvited, to preach at the seminary where I had been trained. This seminary had been a predominantly affirming and life-giving institution in the years when I was there, but in recent years the administration grew increasingly conservative and narrow in its regard of women.

And maybe I fostered a doubt or two about this thing called "The Ministry" when, on my first Sunday as pastor of Calvary Baptist Church in Waco, my family and all of the other worshipers had to pass through a line of thirty picket-waving protesters in order to enter the church building. I remember our seven-year-old son Taylor squeezing my hand and whispering, "Mom, who is Jezebel and why are they calling you that?"[3]

Have women been poorly advised about entering the pastoral ministry? Or, if we listened to God's Spirit and chose this path of our own volition, were we just plain nuts? The truth is, if I answer *yes* to either of the above questions on any given day (and sometimes I do), I likely will have recanted by nightfall. Such is my ongoing love-hate relationship with the pastorate. I am still in the process of discovering what it means to be a child of God and a pastor and a woman all at the same time. My purpose in these pages is to share something of my own experience as I've navigated the sometimes turbulent waters of Baptist tradition in following the call of Jesus upon my life.

ROOTS

I come from southern stock. Both my mother and father were born and raised in Birmingham, Alabama. My father's father was a coal miner; my mother's father was a mine inspector. As a young man my father left Alabama and enlisted in the Air Force, where he served for twenty-four years as a boom operator. My mother worked as a stay-at-home mom, then as a secretary, then, after completing her college degree, as a middle-school teacher.

My mom, who'd been raised in the Methodist tradition in Birmingham, made a profession of faith and was baptized in a Baptist church at the age of twenty-one while we were stationed in Bermuda. From that time forward my mother, my brother, and I attended a Baptist church in every place our family was stationed, though we were never very particular about the "brand." Along the way we attended an Independent Baptist church, a couple of American Baptist churches, and a number of Southern Baptist churches. I remember one particularly strict Baptist church that required my mother to sign an agreement to refrain from movies, dancing, and miniskirts in order to be allowed to teach children's Sunday school. Even in our denominational ignorance we knew that this was over the top, and we stayed there only a few months. I made my profession of faith and was baptized at the age of nine in a small Baptist church in Orlando, Florida.

My brother and I got used to the rhythm of moving to a new city every four or five years during our childhood. The years we spent in the San Joaquin valley of California when I was in junior high and high school were some of the most formative of my life. Even as a young teenager, I recognized the freedom in California from many of the more provincial attitudes I'd witnessed in the South, particularly with regard to gender roles. The memories of my positive experience in California would later draw me back to the West Coast when I decided to enter seminary.

FAITH METAMORPHOSIS

While I was in college in Louisiana my father made the decision to retire from military service, and our family moved back to Orlando. I joined a large Southern Baptist church with an active college ministry and plunged right in. It was during a trip to Israel with the church's college choir that I made a commitment to follow Jesus in earnest. It just so happened that in that particular church at that time, following Jesus in earnest automatically meant going to seminary—it was just the "spiritual" thing to do. So, six months after graduating from college I went—without any notion of where seminary might lead and without any clear sense of a "call" to a particular ministry. I got on a plane with eleven dollars in my pocket and I headed back to California, this time to the San Francisco Bay Area.

Golden Gate Baptist Theological Seminary (GGBTS) was a good home for me and offered a wonderful theological education (the incident in preaching class notwithstanding). I was unprepared, however, for the confusion I felt at meeting for the first time various women who claimed to be called to pastoral ministry. My conservative religious upbringing never allowed for that possibility. One of my earliest memories of seminary life is of traipsing down the hall of my dormitory to the prayer room every morning at 6:30 AM. There I would get on my knees and pray for all of the poor, misguided women in my classes who thought God was calling them to be pastors! My "God box" simply wasn't big enough for such a notion. But over time, and through dialogue and friendship with professors, administrators, and students at GGBTS, God began to open up some sky over my faith. I began to see God and the Bible and the church in new ways. My own understanding of myself also began to change, and it was an utterly invigorating time for me—a renaissance of faith.

Joan Chittister, a Catholic nun, wrote some words that aptly describe what happened in me during my seminary experience.

The soul only grows as a result of the changes that tax and test our tolerance for the present, of the ability to find God where God is rather than where we think God should be for us. Change of mind, change of heart, change of hopes, change of insights require us over and over again to sort through all the pseudo-certainties of our lives, keeping some things, altering others, discarding the rest of the notions that were once its convictions, its absolutes, the very staples of our souls.[4]

MINISTRY BEGINNINGS

I joined a remarkable church in San Francisco, Nineteenth Avenue Baptist Church (NABC), a multicultural, multicongregational church with a strong heart for marginalized people and a vibrant, caring fellowship. Shortly after my arrival, the congregation asked me to serve as their part-time music minister. In the months that followed, the pastor of NABC and my mentor, Bill Smith, gently prodded me along, giving me opportunities to preach and to give pastoral care in addition to my music responsibilities. Upon my graduation from seminary, NABC asked me to stay on as the associate pastor, and several years later I became their pastor. In all, I served with Nineteenth Avenue Church for fourteen years. I owe them a huge debt of gratitude for everything they taught me about what it means to pastor a congregation.

In January 1998, as I made breakfast in my kitchen in San Francisco one morning, the telephone rang. It was the chair of the pastor search committee from Calvary Baptist Church in Waco, Texas, asking if I would send them my resumé. Daniel Vestal, Coordinator for the Cooperative Baptist Fellowship, had suggested my name to them as a possible candidate. Without strong leanings toward this particular church, but also not wanting to close a door prematurely, I sent my resumé, which led to a conversation, and then to another conversation and another, and four months later our family was flying to Texas to meet the congregation. On 31 May 1998, Calvary called me to be their pastor by a vote of 190-73.

To say that this was a big step for this congregation is a huge understatement. Calvary was in no way the congregation everyone assumed would be the first Baptist church in Texas to call a female pastor. I think they surprised even themselves. In fact, when the search committee began to realize that the process might lead them to me, it caused them a momentary panic. Calvary, while clearly having a progressive vein running through it (the church has been supportive of the Cooperative Baptist Fellowship since its inception and has had women deacons and women on the pastoral staff for years), has typically been rather traditional and somewhat conservative in its make-up. But this, to me, makes their action all the more meaningful.

Calvary had no "agenda" to fulfill or a desire to gain notoriety by calling a woman as their pastor; they simply were responding to the leading of the Spirit. This is not to say that my coming was without pain or controversy. Approximately fifty people left the congregation in the days following my call. Since 1998, Calvary has grown in a variety of ways. Still, it took us a while to find our "rhythm" as pastor and congregation, and the first couple of years were challenging.

THE SBC AMENDMENTS

My call to Calvary in the summer of 1998 coincided with the Southern Baptist Convention's adoption of the "Family Amendment" to the *1963 Baptist Faith and Message* (*BF&M*) calling wives to "submit graciously to the servant leadership" of their husbands. Two years later the SBC further amended the *BF&M* declaring, among other things, that "the office of pastor is limited to men as qualified by Scripture."

Because theological and biblical responses to these two amendments are offered elsewhere in this book, I am limiting in this chapter my own biblical and theological observations about these declarations, focusing instead on the ways in which I have chosen to live and to follow my calling in their wake.

One of the deepest flaws in the *1998* and *2000 Baptist Faith and Message* amendments, in my opinion, is that the amendments are based on a few selected verses in Scripture that are largely *descriptive* of first-century culture, but that have been interpreted in such a way as to be *prescriptive* for all successive centuries and peoples and cultures. This interpretive approach was clearly inadequate with regard, for example, to the issue of slavery, and it is inadequate regarding the issue of women as well. Be that as it may, the amendments now exist and have become embedded in the mortar of Southern Baptist life. There is nothing I can do to change that fact, but I *do* have choices about how I will follow Christ and about what kind of person and minister I will endeavor to be.

I love the Bible. I believe that Scripture is an indispensable tool for knowing the heart of God and learning the ways of Christ. As followers of Jesus we are not at liberty to play "fast and loose" with the Bible—quite the opposite! We must use every resource available to us, along with the guiding presence of the Spirit, to interpret Scripture responsibly and faithfully. After twenty years of studying, discussing, praying over, and wrestling with the teachings of Scripture, I have come to understand that I am a pastor, *not in spite of what the Bible says, but because of what the Bible says.*

SOME THINGS I'M LEARNING

Pastors, both male and female, come in as many different packages as the churches who call them. My experience with the pastorate is just that—my own experience. No two stories are alike, but there are some things I've been learning along the way that may be helpful to some as they respond to their own obstacles and challenges in following the call of Jesus into vocational ministry.

Fundamentalism. I have no fondness for fundamentalism in any of its rigid forms. But my own personal journey has reminded me to be more patient with fundamentalist *people* who see things differently than I do. I'm embarrassed today by the narrow beliefs I unquestioningly adopted as a teenager and young adult. But God clearly wasn't through with me then, nor is God through with me yet, so who's to say God is through with anyone else? That is not to say that people are enlightened only when they arrive at my conclusions. But as long as a body is breathing, that body has the opportunity to make some new response to God, and giving up on someone—anyone—is always premature.

At the same time, we have a limited number of days on this earth. We may spend them for good or for ill. We may spend them fearfully or faithfully, but we must choose one or the other. There came a day in my twenties when it dawned on me that I wasn't going to be able to make everyone happy—that there would always be someone who didn't understand my call or someone who categorically opposed my call. I realized that ultimately I have to listen to God's voice. A decade later there came the realization that I had, for some time, stopped considering myself a Southern Baptist. That was a freeing moment and I have not looked back.

Anger. I've come to some convictions about anger, and here I tread lightly. I weep sometimes when I hear or read about the pain and humiliation some women have borne, particularly in religious life. When doors are slammed in your face; when your gifts are repeatedly discounted and dismissed; when church history and theology and ecclesiology together seem to gang up on you, the effects can be devastating. I have experienced some of that anguish—maybe more than some, not nearly as much as others.

I'm rarely more frustrated than when someone tries to pay me a compliment by saying, "You're not one of those angry feminists." In the first place, I *am* a feminist—or as I prefer to say, an *equalist*. Feminism means different things to different people. I like the way Christian writer Sonja Curry-Johnson defines the word:

> To call oneself a feminist . . . is to celebrate and explore all that is woman—not to defame or emasculate all that is man. When a woman insists upon being treated as a living, thinking human being, while also standing up for the rights of all her sisters—how can this be interpreted as threatening by anyone but the most ignorant of people?[5]

Another reason I bristle when someone assures me that I'm not an "angry feminist" is that this particular comment is horribly dismissive of the legitimate anger of many women, the shoes of whom the well-meaning person obviously has never walked in. I remember a friend from the seventies who said one day in an exasperated voice, "They tell me I'm not an 'uppity Black'—as if that's supposed to flatter me!" We must never presume to know more than we do about what lies behind another person's anger or pain. Sometimes anger is the most appropriate response to injustice and the best motivating tool for action.

However, while I wholly believe that anger sometimes can propel us toward a healthy and necessary behavior, anger will also kill us from the inside if we choose to build a home there. Again, it comes down to the brevity of life and choosing how one is going to spend one's days. The following are means by which I have tried to stay sane and emotionally healthy as a pastor.

Humor. First, I try to employ a liberal dose of humor whenever possible. So much of what people have said and done is too ludicrous not to laugh! I love to write, and sometimes it helps me to step outside of my immediate, painful experience and to become a biographer of my own life, recording stories that still make me laugh. For instance, I'm reminded of the letter I received shortly after the SBC adopted the *2000 BF&M*. One irate gentleman wrote a letter to me, but began with a note directed at my husband, Tim:

First allow me to address the subordinated marriage partner of that would-be leader of a Baptist Church in Waco, Texas, i.e. the depressingly-hyphenated Ms. Julie Pennington-Russell—whose last name says all there is to say about her subscription to yet another passage of scripture which goes something like this: '*Wives, submit to your husbands . . . .*' I shall pray for you this day, MISTER Pennington-Russell, because you are obviously in dire need of it.

I couldn't make that stuff up if I tried! Some of it is as hilarious as it is outrageous, and it's great material for the book I'll probably write someday. It's all grist for the mill.

Fills Me, Drains Me. Second, I try to seek out and surround myself with people who keep my emotional balloon up in the air. One of the best pieces of advice I ever received was from another friend and mentor, Hardy Clemons, who told me of a device he's used for years in the quest to stay emotionally balanced. He said, "Julie, when you're making appointments for the coming week, get in the habit of putting an initial next to the person's name. Write either an *F* or a *D*. *F* stands for *Fills* me—*D* stands for *Drains* me. Then just make sure you spend time with a few more people each week who fill you than who drain you, and you'll be OK."[6]

This technique may not work for everyone, but it's important to me to have people in my life who act as agents of grace and encouragement. Incidentally, this is one of the reasons I make no compromise when advising women who are searching for the right seminary. I tell them, "Do not even *look* at a seminary in which a significant majority of the faculty and administration do not demonstrate unambiguous support of your call to ministry. A person's seminary experience is too foundational to waste time with such nonsense. Get on with your call . . . get on with your life."

Friends and Enemies. Third, I try not to confuse my friends with my enemies. There really are people out there who are trying to be supportive and are trying to help in the best way they know how—not always perfectly, not always going about it in the way I would, perhaps, but doing the best they can. Everyone has his or her own cultural or generational baggage to deal with regarding any number of subjects. Ultimately it is counterproductive if

I denigrate or dismiss someone for not being as far along as I think she or he should be regarding women's issues. I appreciate it more than I can say when someone assumes the best in me. I try to do the same for others—not always successfully—but I try.

Choosing What's Most Important. Fourth, I try to choose carefully the battles I am called to fight. It's important to me not to diffuse the impact I *am* able to make by trying to defend every hill. The thing is, you have to know yourself in some significant ways before it becomes clear what *is* and *is not* important to you, and this takes both time and prayer. I've been in ministry for nearly twenty years, and only now is it becoming clear that the two things that matter most to me are having a healthy family life and helping to mobilize churches and individuals to make the best possible difference in the world for Christ's sake. In order to say yes to these, however, I've had to say no to a host of other opportunities.

When I first came to Texas I was overwhelmed by the warm and effusive welcome I received from people around the state. Immediately invitations began to come to serve on committees and to lead this retreat or to speak at that meeting. While I deeply appreciated the support, especially after my experiences in California, I quickly realized that were I to accept even half of these invitations, the congregation who had called me in the first place would never see their pastor! Ironically, many female pastors are discovering that paying attention to our families and churches may be the best contribution we can make to broader Baptist life and to the cause of women ministers. I call it the Nike approach. Rather than lead seminars on why women should be pastors, just *do* it . . . and do it well.

A Big Enough Cause. In the end, it helps to remember that leading a balanced, sane life is not enough. Keeping all of our emotional ducks in a row is not enough. Neither is being ordained, or being called by a church, or sticking it to the Southern Baptist Convention, or gaining personal notoriety. Any of these things may bring momentary satisfaction, but none of them is a goal sufficient enough to order our lives around. William James said happiness is found in giving ourselves to a big enough cause. Fortunately for us, Christ is eager to give us one. *Follow me,* said Jesus. *Love God with all of your heart, soul, mind and strength, and love other people as you love yourself.* There is a greatness in that calling! Every tick of the clock invites us to give back an answer worthy of the One whose purposes are boundless, and whose calling is joy and life and love. No amendment, declaration, or decree has the power to keep any child of God from wrapping his or her life around the mission of Christ as the Spirit leads. Ultimately, the choice is ours. ✝

NOTES

[1] Frederick Buechner, *The Alphabet of Grace* (New York: Harper Collins, 1970), 40-41.

[2] I learned later that this professor was quoting the 18th-century British writer Samuel Johnson, to whom this phrase is attributed.

[3] It should be noted that none of the protesters were from Waco. A group of about thirty had traveled from East Texas for the occasion.

[4] Joan Chittister, O.S.B., *The Fire in These Ashes* (Kansas City: Sheed & Ward, 1995), 78-79.

[5] Sonja Curry-Johnson, "Weaving an Identity Tapestry," *Listen Up: Voices from the Next Feminist Generation*, ed. Barbara Findlen (Seattle: Seal Press, 1995), 221.

[6] It is probably best not to make it known that you use this system, for it tends to make people with whom you have appointments a bit paranoid.

CHAPTER THREE

The Female of the Species

Charles Wellborn

One Sunday morning several months ago I visited a small church located near where I live. The church met in a simple building and less than a hundred people were present for the service.

I felt comfortable and much at home. The hymns were familiar and the congregation sang enthusiastically. After the offering was collected, we stood and sang the Doxology. The minister preached a clear, concise sermon dealing with a basic facet of the Christian gospel, the meaning of the cross. At the conclusion of the sermon we sang a hymn of invitation. Two people responded to the call for commitment. A woman, already a Christian, came forward to place her membership in the church. A mature man made his profession of faith in Christ as his Savior.

I went away that morning satisfied. I had found what I needed and wanted—a genuine experience of worship and an encounter with the Spirit of God. But I also knew that there was something strikingly different about the service, something that after years of churchgoing, I was largely unaccustomed to. The preacher (and pastor) that morning was a gray-haired, sprightly woman. With fire in her bones and conviction in her voice she had preached the gospel—but, still, she was a female. For me, that was different.

I left that service musing, somewhat sadly, on the undeniable fact that many of our contemporary Christian denominations are violently divided on the issue of women in the pulpit. The Church of England, for instance, faces factional division because of its willingness to accept women pastors. My own denomination, Southern Baptist, has officially adopted a statement of faith that bars such women as I heard that day from the pastorate. She, and her congregation, would be anathema.

The issue of women in the pulpit is not a new one. It has bedeviled the Christian community for centuries. I have been involved in discussions about this question with fellow pastors where there have been condescending remarks about the abilities of women in the pulpit. I have been reminded of the tongue-in-cheek comment of the eighteenth-century polymath, Samuel Johnson, who is reported to have said, "A woman's preaching is like a dog's walking on its hinder legs. It is not done well, but you are surprised to find it done at all." I dare say that Dr. Johnson, who was not a stupid man, might well have altered his opinion had he attended with me the service to which I alluded earlier in this article.

Inevitably, when I discuss this matter with my fundamentalist Christian friends, they will point to biblical passages that they believe support their point of view. I deeply respect that approach. Like them, I am a Bible-believing Christian. I accept the teachings of the Bible as an authoritative guide in matters of Christian faith and practice. But there is a basic difference between us.

While I understand and accept the Bible to be the written revelation of God's character and will, I do not give final or infallible authority to any human or organizational interpretation of the meaning of those Scriptures, whether that interpretation be the idea of any individual or the pronouncements adopted by a show of hands in an assembly or convention. Christians do not, or should not, worship a particular method of biblical interpretation; they worship the God who is revealed in the Bible—and the difference is important. The Scriptures are the written word, but the meaning of the words must always be understood and interpreted, and in this task there is a more important Word. The Apostle John declares in the beginning of his Gospel, "In the beginning was the Word, and the Word was with God, and the Word was God" (John 1:1). Obviously, John is not speaking here of the written word but of the Logos, the living Word, the Christ. That living Word is our final authority when it comes to matters of meaning and interpretation. Jesus said, "He who has seen me has seen the Father" (John 14:9). All of our scriptural exegesis must be undertaken in the shadow of the Logos, and we are not entitled to interpret particular passages of Scripture in ways that are inconsonant with the character and message of Christ. Every passage of Scripture must be viewed through a singular prism. That prism is the Christ as revealed to us in the Scripture.

In the Southern Baptist gathering that adopted a resolution excluding women from the pulpit and the pastorate, one of its leaders is reported to have said, "If a woman claims she had been called to the pastorate, she is simply wrong. She has not been called. God does not contradict himself." While I disagree profoundly with the first part of that statement, I give my hearty "Amen" to the second part. God certainly does not contradict himself. It is precisely for that reason that I find the exclusion of women from pastoral ministry impossible to accept.

Many years ago, when I was a young student in a conservative Baptist seminary, I was taught certain basic principles of exegesis—the discipline of scriptural interpretation. Men like Ray Summers, Robert Daniel, Stewart Newman, and T. B. Maston—names that will ring a bell with some of my older Baptist readers—instructed me in ways of understanding Scripture that have served me well for over fifty years. I see no reason to desert those principles now.

One basic exegetical principle is that for a particular interpretation of a passage of Scripture, one must look at the whole of Scripture and its portrait of the character of God. In applying this principle we must take account of the fact that there is nothing in the Gospels, recounting the ministry of Jesus, that supports the idea that females are second-class citizens of the kingdom of God. Indeed, in his treatment of women, Jesus never discriminated in any way. It is quite clear that women were then, as they have always been, key figures in the Jesus movement. This is especially true in Luke's Gospel where the female followers of Jesus receive particular mention—Joanna, Susanna, and Mary Magdalene, women who traveled with Jesus and the male disciples, fully incorporated in the group.

Of course, Mary Magdalene is the most important of the female disciples, and in John's Gospel she is presented as a model of discipleship. She is, in a real sense, the apostle to the apostles, for she is the first to witness the resurrected Jesus at the tomb on Easter morning, and she is commissioned by the risen Lord to tell the other disciples that she has seen him (John 20). Long into the Middle Ages Mary Magdalene was revered as "apostolorum apostle," apostle to the apostles. Jesus accepted and treated males and females equally, and in this respect he clearly reflects the character of God.

The Apostle Paul reinforced this understanding of the character of God in one of his most forthright declarations, a passage of Scripture not often cited by those who wish to exclude females from the pulpit. In the Epistle to the Galatian church Paul emphatically avers that "There is neither Jew nor

Greek, there is neither bond nor free, there is neither male nor female, for you are all one in Jesus Christ" (Gal 3:28). What the Apostle says here is absolutely consistent with the nature of God as revealed through Jesus Christ.

The God revealed to us through the living Word is one who makes no distinctions on the basis of gender. We often address God in our prayers as "Our Father," and I have no objection to that because it rightly emphasizes the caring concern of God. But that address in no way implies that God is a male sexual being. God transcends any sexual differentiation. In the same way that God is not black, white, yellow, red, American, Russian, Chinese, or African, God is neither male nor female. Medieval (male) artists pictured God as an old man with a long, white beard, but that is a totally inadequate presentation. By tradition, we use the male pronoun for God, but in the fundamental sense God wipes away all gender discrimination.

In the basic matter of salvation God certainly does not make such distinctions. Without regard to gender, or any other human difference, we are all equally invited to come to God. Indeed, it is this refusal on the part of God to make such distinctions, reinforced by the identical characteristics in the teaching of Jesus, that has enabled the Christian faith to make such a significant contribution to the ongoing struggle in the secular society about us against unfair discrimination on the basis of such factors as race and gender.

It is ironic that some Christians should uphold, within the church, a dictum that in effect makes females second-class citizens of the kingdom of God. The Christian affirmation that there can be no gender distinction has been a prime factor in the advance of our secular culture to the position that the majority of that culture holds today: males and females alike are entitled to equal treatment in every part of our society. I do not believe, though I cannot know for sure, that my Christian friends who disagree with me on this issue would support unfair discrimination against women in the marketplace. I do not think they would countenance unequal pay for equal work on the basis of gender or the exclusion of women from positions of leadership in business or government simply because they are female. Yet, do they not realize that when the Christian church endorses this kind of gender discrimination within its own ranks, it unwittingly, perhaps, undergirds those in the secular society who would carry on such practices?

My teachers taught me a second basic principle of exegesis. This was the principle of consistency. If one is to interpret Scripture correctly, one must at the very least be consistent. If, for instance, one approaches Scripture with the conviction that every admonition of the Apostle Paul in the Epistles establishes a permanent and unchanging pattern for church practice, one is not entitled to pick and choose, selecting those parts of Scripture that are seen to be lasting definitions of Christian practice and those that are not. I cannot make this principle of exegesis fit the kind of interpretation that seems to be ordinary among my disagreeing Christian brethren. One of the most frequently cited Scriptural passages by my friends to support their position is 1 Corinthians 14:34. In that passage Paul says, "Let your women keep silent in the churches, for it is not permitted unto them to speak." Leaving aside the seemingly clear meaning of that passage to forbid women having any verbal part in church affairs, whether in the pulpit or not, that seems to settle the matter for my friends. But, if we are to be consistent, we must remember that in that same letter, Paul instructs his hearers just as clearly that "every woman that prays or prophesies with her head uncovered dishonors her head" (1 Cor 11:5). Doesn't this quite evidently mean that a woman who prays or prophesies (preaches) with her head covered is doing a perfectly honorable thing?

Can we ignore the fact that the Apostle in his first letter to Timothy instructs the people to whom he is writing that "women adorn themselves in modest apparel, with shamefulness and sobriety; not with braided hair, or gold, or costly array" (2:9)? In my long life in the church I have heard numerous sermons in which the preacher declared that women were not fit to be pastors or preachers, but I have never heard a sermon in which the preacher ordered his female listeners, on the basis of the Bible, to wear hats when they came to church, or to throw away the gold wedding rings their husbands had given them, or to discard the pearl necklaces given to them in love by their children, or not to commit the sin of coming to church with braided hair. Where is the consistency here? Why pick one admonition and ignore the rest?

At this point my friends argue that because God has assigned individuals differing roles in the church because of gender differences, Paul's instructions concerning women must be understood in a different way from his other pronouncements. I can understand that argument up to a point. There are obvious physical and genetic differences between males and females, as God has created us. Males sire children; females bear children. That is undeniable. But, for the life of me, I have been unable to find any genetic or biological difference between males and females that supports the idea that men are, by virtue of their maleness, better preachers or pastors than women.

In my life I have known good male preachers and poor ones. I am sure that there are good female preachers and poor ones, but the difference is not genetic or sexual. Our individual callings from God to vocation are a matter of our individual talents and the degree of our surrender to the will of God. Some (both male and female) are called to preach; others are called to be missionaries; and others are called to be lay witnesses. The call of God extends to all human beings. It seems to me the height of spiritual arrogance for a male preacher to say that if a pious, dedicated woman understands God's call to her to be that of the ministry, he in his male role has the right to say that she is mistaken and wrong.

The third basic principle of exegesis that I learned was that one must always look at a particular passage of Scripture within its context. It is important to know when the passage was written and to whom it was written. Paul wrote his Epistles to particular Christian communities, operating within their own cultural context. Much of the body of the Epistles deals with fundamental issues in the understanding of Christian doctrine, but also much of Paul's writing is pastoral and practical advice on the special problems each of these communities faced. In approaching the exegesis of these passages we must always keep in mind Paul's primary purpose—the effective witness to the central truths of the gospel.

Perhaps the most instructive passage in this regard is Paul's advice to the Corinthian church regarding the eating of meats that had been offered to idols. Clearly, this was a problem peculiar to the Corinthians. Paul first makes it clear that there is no sin in eating such meat (1 Cor 8:8), then he gives his practical advice: "But take heed lest by any means this liberty of yours becomes a stumbling block to them that are weak" (8:9). His final counsel is "If meat make my brother to offend, I will eat no meat" (8:13).

If we apply our understanding of this passage to the interpretation of other such passages in the Epistles, certain things are clear. First, in dealing with secondary matters of practice within the church, Paul's governing concern is what will further the cause of gospel witness. Second, in dealing with such matters Paul was willing, in his own day and time and in consideration of the pagan culture around him, to advise that the church adopt certain practices, not because there was any sin involved nor, I think, to lay down patterns for the future church, but to avoid offending unnecessarily that particular culture.

It is from this standpoint that I think we can better understand many of Paul's other admonitions to particular churches. Writing to another church in a somewhat different cultural situation, as I have previously mentioned, Paul advised the women in the church in Corinth not to appear in church with their heads uncovered, not to wear gold ornaments or jewelry, and not to braid their hair. Clearly, those practices, though morally neutral in themselves, would in Corinth have been hindrances to their witness. It must be remembered that in this same letter Paul advised women to keep silent in church.

When we seek to understand the cultural situation of the New Testament church, we must realize that the radical beliefs and practices of the church created a tremendous tension in its relationship with the pagan, predominantly Roman ethos in which it operated. The deeply egalitarian teachings of Jesus (the promise of salvation for all) totally contradicted the values of a hierarchical society, economically based on the labor of slaves. A vital part of that pagan society's structure was the subjugated and inferior position of women.

Christianity decisively challenged those pagan values. The Christian church not only allowed but also positively encouraged all human beings—slave and free, Jew and Gentile, educated and uneducated, men and women—to worship, live, and love together. It was especially this facet of the new faith that drew the scorn of Celsius, a prominent second-century pagan critic, who poured vitriolic scorn on Christians for such practices.

Jane Shaw, a widely respected church historian, in her McCandless lecture in March 2000 at Georgetown College in Kentucky, pointed out:

> Roman society had very distinct ideas about how a virtuous woman should behave; submissively, and certainly not speaking in public. Roman law held that by nature women were the weaker sex, they lacked seriousness, and they therefore required the authority of men (husbands and fathers) over them.
>
> It is surely with an awareness of these pagan surroundings that a sensible exegesis of Paul's strictures against women must be seen. Remembering always the Apostle's primary concern with effective Gospel witness, it is not surprising that, as with eating meat to idols, he would advise particular church congregations not to offend unnecessarily the overwhelmingly male-dominated society in which they operated.
>
> The biblical, historical, and archeological evidence suggests that women held the principal leadership offices, alongside men, for the first three centuries, at least, of Christianity. In many early Christian communities women, as well as men, were deacons, presbyters (priests), bishops (episkopei—overseers), apostles

(missionaries), teachers and prophets. Throughout the New Testament, we get tantalizing glimpses of this reality. When Paul wrote to the Christians in Rome, it is deacon Phoebe who carries his letter to them and thereby introduces Paul to them. She was his patron. He concluded his letter to the Romans by greeting the leaders in the Christian community there, among whom there were many women. Ten out of the twenty-eight whom he greets are women: Prisca, Mary, Tryphena, Persis, Julia, Olympas, the mother of Rufus, the sister of Nercus, and Junia. Especially prominent among these women was Junia, "prominent among the apostles," with her husband, Andronicus, whom Paul had known when he was in prison.

Dr. Shaw continues:

> Paul says . . . in his first letter to Timothy, in which he describes a bishop or overseer as being like a householder—he must manage his household well . . . for if someone does not know how to manage his household, how can he take care of God's church? In this letter Paul assumes that the householder is male, but his own travels and missionary activities had shown him otherwise. For example, when he arrived in Philippi, as recounted in Acts 16, he preached to a woman named Lydia, a dealer in purple cloth, a woman of reasonably substantial means and a householder. When she converted to Christianity, so the rest of her household was baptized too (Acts 16:15). And when Paul was released from prison, as recounted at the end of chapter 16 (verse 40), it was to Lydia's house that he went, so that he could meet and worship with other Christians before he left the city.

Actually, this pattern of essential female involvement in the church has continued through the centuries, despite great pressure from the male-dominated society in which it has existed. I know from my own experience as a pastor that no modern church could function without the dedicated efforts of Christian women. We have traditionally entrusted them to teach our children in Sunday school the fundamentals of the Christian faith. They have volunteered by thousands to be missionaries on the home and foreign fields. True, Paul advised the Corinthian church not only that women should keep silent in churches, but that, if women want to learn anything, they should "ask their husbands at home" (1 Cor 14:35). Incidentally, in fifty years I have never heard a sermon on that text. In actual fact several of the finest Bible teachers and expositors I have heard have been women, including a marvelous woman who taught for many years a mixed Bible class of men and women in the church I pastored. My sister, Faye Robbins, is a gifted teacher of the Scripture, and her ministry in various churches has through the years been blessed and productive. The arbitrary exclusion of females from the offices of preacher and pastor does not, for all these reasons and many more, make sense to me.

I think the final and perhaps most decisive point to be made in this argument is to go back to the Apostle Paul himself. As I have repeatedly pointed out, Paul was governed in all his actions by one decisive consideration: the effective witness to the gospel. Paul lived and wrote in a male-dominated society. He was willing, for the sake of the gospel, to make certain concessions to that culture.

We live today in totally different cultural surroundings. The secular culture, with which we have to deal as Christians, is one that is, at least in its majority opinion, committed to sexual and gender equality. We should rejoice in that. Christians have helped to bring that about. Now, if we apply Paul's guiding principle, we must decide what will most effectively serve the cause of Christian witness. To maintain the stance of gender discrimination within the church, it seems to me, seriously harms our witness. On this basis I dare say that the counsel of Paul to the Corinthian church would be very different from the counsel he would give to the church in Nashville or Atlanta or Dallas.

I cannot close without another reference to the worship experience I described in the opening paragraphs of this article. When the gospel is preached and when the Holy Spirit evidently blesses that proclamation with the salvation of a soul, who will label that experience "un-Christian" simply because the preacher was a woman?

Protestants do not, unlike their Catholic brethren, pick out particular individuals in their history and designate them as "saints." But if, in particular, Baptists did have saints, I think the list would include Lottie Moon and Annie Armstrong, two intrepid Christian missionaries for whom annual missions offerings are named. I should imagine that if by some miracle Annie Armstrong and Lottie Moon were to return to us in the flesh, it would be a brave and, I think, foolish pastor who would deny them his pulpit to tell their stories and give their witness, even though they are quite clearly "females of the species." +

CHAPTER FOUR

Still a Baptist Woman

Gladys S. Lewis

I am a Baptist because of my captivity, my exodus, and my pilgrimage. My captivity status helps me understand being human and defines me; my exodus experience helps me recognize the divine and shapes me; and my pilgrimage formation helps me synthesize the human and the divine and identifies me. Being Baptist puts those interpretative strategies in my power because of basic Baptist adherence to soul liberty and soul competency in the captivity; individual freedom in Bible study and prayer in the exodus; and priesthood of the believer and church autonomy in the pilgrimage.

CAPTIVITY

Captivity is our basic human orientation. It describes our natural condition and provides a way to understand and define our life condition. The Old Testament overflows with allusions to being carried away captive, taking captives, and becoming captives. Bondage is a principal preoccupation. The overarching captivity analogy in accounts of the literal bondage of Israel in Egypt grants a bedrock for understanding Old and New Testament worlds.

We are also captive in other ways. Paul writes about captivity, "but I see another law in my members, warring against the law of my mind, and bringing me into captivity to the law of sin which is in my members" (Rom 7:23). In spite of all the varieties of bondage, there is a positive side to captivity that elevates our dismal condition. We meet it first in Isaiah 61:1 and again when Jesus goes to the synagogue and reads from the scroll after his captivity-shattering encounter with Satan on temptation mount:

> The Spirit of the Lord God is upon me; because the Lord has anointed me to preach good tidings unto the meek; he has sent me to bind up the brokenhearted, to proclaim liberty to the captives, and the opening of the prison to them that are bound. (Luke 4:18)

We are not simply a herd of cattle in a pen. We are individuals so worthy of saving that a living God is engaged in our redemption.

That kind of importance defines us spiritually. That kind of individual worth also defines us culturally, a nation of individualists from our beginning. The first prolonged collision the New England colonists suffered with the Native Americans occurred in spring 1675. King Philip's War, as the two-year guerrilla battles were known, ended a half-century of cordial coexistence between the English settlers and the Algonquin tribes of southern New England. Metacomet, the Wampanoag chief dubbed Philip by the colonists, hated the colonists and resented their high-handed ways and incursion on tribal lands.

In February 1676, a group of Narragansetts raided Lancaster, Massachusetts, a frontier community with about fifty families. Many were killed and others taken captive for ransom. Among the captives was Mary White Rowlandson (c. 1635–c. 1678), a daughter of one of the town's founders and wife of its clergyman. Eleven weeks later, just before the war ended, she was ransomed and reunited with her husband and two remaining children after twenty stages of flight, or "removes," as the Narragansetts moved through Massachusetts into Vermont, New Hampshire, and back. During those weeks, she endured unimaginable suffering.

A couple of years later, Rowlandson recorded the narrative of her captivity and it became immensely popular because it served her readers on so many literary, spiritual, and psychological levels. It was a lay sermon by a woman, a spiritual autobiography, and an amazing adventure tale. Her narrative does what captivity tales always do. The captive defines self in contrast to the captivity culture, and, if redeemed, returns to the prior community to share what was learned. We receive rich imagery from the Puritans in the concept of a mission into the wilderness and identity with the land. The promised land that the Israelites in exile sought, by transference in the Puritan colonial's mind, became the New Israel in the New World. The Bible reinforced their experience of boundaries, wilderness, land, captivity, exile, and return.

Mary Rowlandson's captivity narrative birthed a principal literary genre in American writing that comes straight from a biblical model. But captivity is far more than a literary genre that serves as a communication device. Captivity provides a metaphoric construct for our individual and group experience in that we learn from our suffering, or we are destroyed by it.

And there is more. Culturally, women have been captives of patriarchal institutions. Captivity is not new. We have a grammar of captivity in our past, our present, and our future. The Fundamentalists and their overt program of exclusion is debilitating and embarrassing, but it is not new. In many ways, it is more honest in the present than that captivity we have known in the past. But we can turn all of it to our advantage. We will never be free from the captivity that surrounds and threatens, but we can make it more negotiable, more pragmatically useful, if we learn from marginal experience and teach our communities.

Current rules and dicta don't affect us as Baptists moving in soul liberty and soul competency. A free and competent Baptist can survive the wilderness captivity. I am still Baptist because soul competency allows me to work out my own faith positions when life gives me conditions not covered by doctrine. We are all Catholics pragmatically. We want someone to make the rules, tell us how to live in them, bless us when we succeed, and correct us with assignments for extra credit when we fail. In Baptist circles right now, we call that Fundamentalism, but it is a Catholic position by ecclesiology, and it is Fascist politically. The trouble with that kind of rigidity comes when life dishes up a serving of something without rules for solutions. I live daily where nothing of faith markers has been mapped. Soul liberty and competency allow me to be my own cartographer without losing my way on the journey. I learn from my captivity about my humanity. Engagement with my soul in the experience defines my humanity.

EXODUS

My exodus experience helps me recognize the divine and shapes me. When God set Israel free, the people needed forty years to become free before they could go on into their promise. In the "removes," or stages, of the exodus, they learned of God's reality and presence to take the form God intended for them. Usually, we read the exodus from the point of view of Moses, or the people, or the text writers. In Isaiah 51 and 52, we have God's account:

> Hearken unto me, my people . . . for a law shall proceed from me
> . . . The captive exile hastens that he may be loosed . . . But I am
> the LORD thy God, that divided the sea, whose waves roared . . .

And I have put my words in your mouth, and I have covered you in the shadow of my hand, that I may . . . say . . . You are my people . . . I have taken out of your hand the cup of trembling . . . you shall no more drink it again . . . Shake yourself from the dust . . . loose yourself from the bands of your neck . . . Break forth into joy . . . for the LORD has comforted his people.

The New Testament position on our exile condition as Gentiles outside grace beckons us from Ephesians 2:12 and 19: "Remember," Paul says, "that at that time you were without Christ, being aliens from the commonwealth of Israel and strangers from the covenants of promise, having no hope, and without God . . . . So then you are no longer strangers and aliens, but you are citizens with the saints, and also members of the household of God." My exodus experience helps me recognize the divine and it shapes me.

For many years, our family went to Copper Mountain, Colorado, to ski during the interim between Christmas and New Year's when the Physician's Winter Retreat, sponsored by the University of Oklahoma Health Sciences Center, features a continuing medical education forum. In 1993, my surgeon husband, Wilbur, and I arrived two days before Christmas with our children: Karen and her husband, Howard; David, his wife, Sadako, and baby, Jason; Leanne and her husband, Carey; and Cristen.

Wilbur, an excellent skier, was coming down B slope at Copper Mountain, on Monday, 27 December, a bit after 12:30 PM, with Leanne, Carey, and David. The day was somewhat snowy and overcast, so there were no shadows to indicate ridges or other elevations in the terrain or flags to alert skiers. Leanne, in front of the pack, went right and took off her skis to go in to lunch. Wilbur followed her, but turned to the left. Just a few steps from the door to the inn was a drainage ditch with a culvert into it, making a slight elevation that did not create a shadow. Because it was not flagged, Wilbur did not note its presence. He was not going fast, because he was headed toward a snow bank to remove his skis. As he skied over the area, the tips of his skis caught in the elevation and he fell face forward into the ground. The impact caused a ring fracture of his first cervical vertebra and shattered the second one. His injury was the kind often associated with those divers receive. (It is exactly the injury of actor Christopher Reeve.)

Because that area of the spinal cord services autonomic systems of the body, such as breathing, Wilbur was immediately without the ability to breathe. Carey saw the entire scenario and rushed to him, calling for help. David, last in the group, came just after the fall, hurried to help with resuscitation, but watched in panic as he saw his father turning blue. Leanne ran to Wilbur, and he mouthed, "Get help! Get help!" Attending our same conference were a cardiologist and his physician assistant wife who immediately began CPR. The ski patrol came quickly with oxygen and carried Wilbur to the nearby clinic. After emergency attention, he was evacuated to Denver to St. Anthony Central, a trauma center, placed on a ventilator, and diagnosed as quadriplegic: paralyzed from the neck down. His condition was so grave that he was not expected to live through the night. However, when his vital signs and mental condition improved by Tuesday morning, his orthopedist, neurologist, and general surgeon operated.

After his surgeries and several interchanges between his mouthed questions and our carefully explained narratives, he knew exactly his condition and what we faced. Wilbur is a ventilator-dependent quadriplegic, a bleak, grim, dismal reality. We have learned our exodus expulsion was not at the Red Sea; it was at the base of a ski slope in the Colorado Rockies. At that instant around noon, 27 December 1993, our lives were shot into another orbit for as long as we live—an existence of exodus where we live on a plane somewhere between life and death, neither totally one nor the other. Not a day goes by when he does not face death in life, nor I face life in death. We are neither where we were, nor where we are going on the existence level we have been awarded, where we try to marshal our exodus. We go to sleep and wake with Death's arm about our shoulders. We fight on two fronts; his is despair and mine is cynicism. His comes from living on the brink of death. Mine comes from facing the threats to our survival each day, knowing as soon as I solve one set of problems, another will take its place. We have two sides of the same problem: time. He cannot do one thing, and he is oppressed by time. I must do everything, and I am oppressed by time.

So we beg for manna to have nourishment for our paralyzed wanderings. Food comes with prayer and Bible study, but not the kind of devotional exercise I had known in the past. Set apart rituals of spiritual enhancement require time, and I have none. None. For many months, I existed on one to three hours of sleep in twenty-four as I cared for Wilbur, kept my job, and supervised closing his office, managing caregivers, and struggling with financial survival at the hands of people who should have been helping us.

In learning from the exodus, we discover we all have different experiences of grace. One of my grace gifts came the day I realized I could be a spiritual person on the hoof. I could "read" the Bible in my mind and hear God's voice. I could "speak" my thoughts and ideas to God at red lights, and it counted as prayer. My discipline with language helps me at this point. I have so many words in me, good investments I have made of great artists. At any given moment, I can "read" Shakespeare's sonnets, Fitzgerald's *Great Gatsby*, God's New Testament, or my husband's love letters, none of which any of them will ever write again. I love words. I can roll around in them, pull them over my head as a blanket, and be renewed.

When I am locked in linguistic combat with a laboratory, I "read" Shakespeare's "A man can smile and smile and be a villain"; when I recall the days of our other life, I "read" Fitzgerald's benediction on Gatsby, that he drove on to that vision not knowing his dream was behind him; when I think of what I face each day, I "read" Jesus in the Gospels saying, "Take up my yoke and learn of me"; when I finally reach the end of my day, I "read" Wilbur's "To my loving wife." In the process, I have read through a window on all of life experience, and I pray, "Thank you."

What do we learn in our captivity margins of exile and exodus? Wilbur is a captive of his poor, diminished, suffering, petrified body. And so am I. The alienated American cultural subject is the soul we recognize as our own in our particular captivities. Anthropologist Victor Turner's work in studies of people in liminal landscapes examines what happens to groups and individuals with a retreat or forced exile into the marginal, into an existence where the boundary is removed, the exile position. We should feel at home as Baptists in our culture if we understand the secular expression to be a fruition of an ancient correlation between Old Israel and New Israel, as our founders compared themselves. We go into the wilderness for testing and growth. We must look to this current alienation as opportunity for expansion of self, group, and context. When colonial captives were redeemed from captivity, they returned with stories of lessons learned that would benefit the group. Our task as human beings and Baptist women? Learn our stories well and teach them ethically as we learn in the exodus how the divine and human interact to shape us.

Baptists are uniquely equipped to deal with the marginal experience and proving of exodus living because of our historic emphasis on Bible study and prayer. Two weeks ago, I read again Ralph Waldo Emerson's essay, "Self-Reliance," because I had assigned it to a class. I have read that essay a dozen times, but his comments on prayer grasped my mind as never before. He wrote,

> Prayer looks abroad and asks for some foreign addition to come
> through some foreign virtue, and loses itself in endless mazes of

natural and supernatural . . . . Prayer that craves a particular com-
modity—anything less than all good, is vicious. Prayer is the
contemplation of the facts of life from the highest point of view. It
is the soliloquy of a beholding and jubilant soul. It is the spirit of
God, pronouncing His works good. But prayer as a means to effect
a private end, is theft and meanness . . . . As soon as [we] are at one
with God, [we] will not beg. [We] will see prayer in all action . . . .

An exodus lesson? Prayer is not selfish, not an insurance policy for what we
want.

Wilbur suffers especially at night when real darkness joins the other
shadows on life. He wrestles with Jacob's night angel. And so do I. Because I
have wrestled with the angel, I have had to learn how to renegotiate previous
patterns, because I can't walk the same way. We do get the blessing, Wilbur
and I, but blessings come at a price. We are crippled. Coming to grips with
the disintegration of my life as the wife of my husband and the shift in my
position in my family with my husband's injury sabotages these ridiculous
rules that say I must wait on my husband for direction and authority. My
husband is paralyzed and ventilator-dependent. I am our wage earner, business manager, and linchpin. What nonsense to pose as weak and dependent.
I wrestle with the angel in an ambiguous stranglehold. Jacob never saw the
angel's face; we have never seen our angel's face, but we know him. Wilbur
wrestles with the Angel of Death; I wrestle with the Angel of Life—and they
are both God. We are equally blessed, but we remain horribly wounded. And
I am independently wounded with my own pain.

I am woman; I love God; God loves me. In the words of C. S. Lewis, my
"pain is [God's] megaphone." I will not let others define me as an intrusion
before that which I know exists between myself and the One I worship and
move in day by day. *I will not.*

That was a struggle I faced long before the arrival of the current "set of
silly sibilant sayings some sources set before us as sacred." The contemporary
crowd of creed-makers is a bunch of children piping in the market, to use
Jesus' words about immaturity in serious spiritual issues. Baptist women have
a history of facing sophisticated obstacles. This current language is helpful,
in fact. We shrug, smile, and reengage in lives where that mind-set has
absolutely no connection and certainly no collegiality.

In our exodus, I have gained a new attitude and understanding about
Bible study. I am glad I spent all those years on the six-point record system
and study courses and Bible study in Sunday school. But in my current

exodus, I am reading the Bible by the way I live. Remember the Vacation Bible School memorization programs? My two are "Thy word have I hid in my heart that I might not sin against thee" and the watchword "I will do the best I can with what I have for Jesus' sake today." The two go together and must be present for us to survive in the exodus. From my wilderness vantage, I have noticed people do two things with Bible study: they make it a substitute for practical ministry or a substitute for belief. What else can be deduced when people drive miles to a Bible study but won't go across the street to help someone? What else can be deduced when so much language extols its precise merits but not a word offers its spirit?

The Bible is a collection of narratives of violence: murder, betrayal, and brokenness. In our connections with the biblical stories through the collegiality of our own brokenness, we find meaning for our narratives—inspiration from the violence done to us *and* the violence we perpetrate on others. To make the biblical story a totem, an object of worship, or a lucky charm violates its spirit and diminishes its force for healing. It is a road map for our journey, a diary for our reflection, and a compass for our direction: a text with many voices, many narrators, many themes, and many interpretations.

By reading about Jesus in the Bible, we learn a great deal that affirms us spiritually and culturally. Especially as women. Especially about Jesus and non-Jewish women. He first announced his ministry to one: the woman at the well. Jesus never got entangled with doctrine; he lived it, and while living it, he told stories and took care of people. I think this is the edge women have with Jesus. Jesus announced he was the Messiah to a non-Jewish woman. That event came out in a practical ministry setting and conversation—he wanted a drink of water. Of course, the emphasis we get is on his knowing she was a woman with a bad reputation and being kind to her anyway—chalk one up for male rhetoric.

The Syrophoenician woman helped Jesus clarify his ministry by using his language against him. Does the jingo-ism and ethnic chauvinism of Jesus in that passage bother you? After he had fed the multitudes, she came asking him to heal her daughter. He said, "I can't take the children's bread and throw it before dogs." He called her a dog, and I don't think it was because she was not cute. She said, "Dogs eat crumbs under the children's table. I would take those."

Jesus checks himself. I am helped enormously by thinking of Jesus as a teacher. I think Jesus had just restated the syllabus to fifteen freshmen and this Syrophoenician woman graduate student walked up with a real question, and Jesus responded in a tone he wanted to use for the freshmen. But she, knowing how to use language and metaphor, turned it on him. Submissiveness? Bah! Balderdash! My exodus experience helps me recognize the divine and it shapes me.

PILGRIMAGE

My pilgrimage formation helps me synthesize the human and the divine and identifies me. My pilgrimage comes from my salvation story, which rises from being my own priest in spiritual matters. The altar stone in our cherished Baptist belief in the priesthood of the believer is John 3:16: "For God so loved the world [in its captivity, its exodus, and its pilgrimage] that he gave his only Son, so that everyone [every single individual] who believes in him may not perish but may have eternal life."

My salvation story and my service stories all have Baptist bindings. As a seventeen-year-old, I converted to Christianity at the Exchange Avenue Baptist Church in south Oklahoma City in one of those youth-led revivals when OBU student Milton Ferguson (former President of Midwestern Seminary before the purge) was the preacher. Soon afterward, I became a mission volunteer and prepared myself as a nurse. I met Wilbur. We fell in love. (I did. He sort of eased into it, but I knew I had him. I could tell by the little things.) We finished our education, had two babies, spent two terms on the mission field at the Baptist Hospital in Asuncion, Paraguay, had two more babies there, and had to leave because of political shifts in the government that surfaced in the Public Health Ministry, the license granting authority for us.

We have lived in the Oklahoma City area since 1970. Wilbur developed a prominent private surgical practice, was one of the seven original founders of the Baptist Medical-Dental Fellowship, and gave of his total means in service to others—from the Grace Rescue Mission clinic locally to mission hospitals in South America and East Asia. I moved into a role I call my professional Baptist era, and I gave my time, energy, and talent to Baptist churches, Woman's Missionary Union, and Southern Baptist Convention boards. We went all over the world in service capacities through medicine and Baptists. I was on the Committee on Order of Business the year the Fundamentalist takeover occurred. I sat in meetings and listened and knew my days as a woman Baptist in the circles in which I had been traveling had

49

ended. By that time, I also knew that volunteerism, satisfying as it was, could not substitute for professional engagement in a work.

So I returned to study, earned a Master of Arts in English and Creative Writing, and found my niche in academia. I went on to earn a Ph.D. in American and British Literature and have been an English Professor at the University of Central Oklahoma since 1990. All of that had finished, and I had been at my post two years when our accident happened. My work forms a backdrop for our lives and provides the financial means I must have to care for Wilbur as well as maintain my own sense of reality and contribution beyond myself.

Why am I still a Baptist? I am still a Baptist because that is who I am. I was a Baptist long before the current epidemic of theological soul-eating bacteria infected us. Baptist is my name. My life orientation and soul habits have always emanated from that name which identifies me. I suppose I could move into another room in the Lord's house; I could live in the Presbyterian room or the Methodist room or some other. But I am more comfortable with the furniture in the Baptist room. I became a Baptist by choice, and I remain one by choice. That is not to say I have not considered rearranging the furniture or engaging in some more radical activity within those walls, but Baptist I remain, because those parameters help me define my faith system in the most practical manner. In response to being my own priest in salvation matters and being in a church that is autonomous under the will and direction of God, I move forward in my pilgrimage and sharpen my identity.

I was born and given a name. When I converted, I chose a name. When I married, I took another name. All of those names constitute who I am. I will not change; I cannot change. We have Baptist connections, Wilbur and I, and we continue to enjoy a sustaining collegiality with people who share our history.

I am my own agent in salvation matters because we cling to our belief in the *priesthood of the believer*. I work it out with God who has provided the way through Christ. We must not allow current language of disenfranchisement rob us of our history of the struggle—the good old days were good because we had years of experience in subversive success. We knew how to work within the system to make our contributions, fuel our personal sense of mission. When women began to move out of those parameters, you will recall that we were met with resistance. We should do now what we did then: continue to respond to the free-moving Spirit in our hearts, talents, and sensitivity to God's claim on our gifts to respond to God in soul liberty.

I am still a Baptist, because I am part of an *autonomous church*. The emphasis and the New Testament imagery of church always fixes on individuals and their metaphoric analogy as body and body parts to underscore the necessity of cooperative action in our individual reality. Under God, we are free, gifted individuals voluntarily participating in the Body of Christ, the church, to do God's will and honor the Lord. Romans 12:4-5 reads, "For as in one body we have many members, and not all the members have the same function, so we, who are many, are one body in Christ, and individually we are members one of another." And 1 Corinthians 10:17 sketches this portrait for us: "Because there is one bread, we who are many are one body, for we all partake of the one bread." But this community of service never supplants individual worth before God. Galatians 3:26 stresses that fact: "for in Christ Jesus you are all children of God through faith." An individual moves out of captivity, through exile, into pilgrimage as an individual. A church is a group of freed, experienced exiles, helping other strangers bring order to their pilgrimages.

A major problem exists with the current SBC regime's dictating to churches and getting away with it. I am not shocked by the patriarchy in recent SBC resolutions. But I am surprised that Southern Baptist churches have gone along with the trickle-down theology that becomes polarizing in the congregational context. Some of our shameful present comes from religious people's basic insecurity with women, because they are insecure about their own identity and cast that doubt in religious robes. It has always been that way.

My generation was taught that Roger Williams was the great pioneer in soul liberty—the first Baptist who founded Rhode Island, the historians tell us. And he was, but he was taught by a woman, Anne Hutchinson, who challenged the control by early Puritan ministers over individual biblical interpretation. So Mistress Hutchinson held weekly Bible studies in her home and retaught the Bible lessons from the Sunday sermons. Roger Williams was a member of her Monday School Class. I did not learn that in a church or seminary context. I had to go to one of those secular humanist institutions and get a degree in Early American Literature to get the skinny on Mistress Anne Hutchinson. Her story parallels the demonizing of Woman's Missionary Union promoted by, of all groups, the Foreign Mission Board, now the International Mission Board. Her movement, the Antinomian Crisis (meaning against authority, or freedom within authority) is WMU's history. They give us credit for being witches, but not for being principal actors and causative agents in the creation of church history.

51

My pilgrimage formation helps me synthesize the human and the divine and identifies me.

I am a Baptist because of my captivity, my exodus, and my pilgrimage. Because we connect with each other most thoroughly through our stories, I have told you mine, proclaiming as I do, *I am still a Baptist woman.* ✛

CHAPTER FIVE

Biblical Authority, Inerrancy, and Equality

Dan Gentry Kent

Many people who believe the Bible teaches that women are assigned a subordinate position in church, home, and society accuse biblical egalitarians of such things as "not believing the Bible," or at least not being fully committed to the authority of the Bible.

A letter to the editor appeared in the *Baptist Standard*, the newspaper of the Baptist General Convention of Texas. It spoke of "those who hold the Scripture inerrant and its principles binding (such as the husband being head of the wife as Christ is head of the church)."[1] The implication is that it is impossible to harmonize the doctrine of inerrancy and a belief in gender equality.

Is this comparing apples and oranges? Actually, the letter quoted and the title of this article deal with two completely different issues, and we need to be careful not to confuse the two.

Inerrancy is a doctrinal position, a conviction regarding the nature of the Bible. A belief in the equality of male and female, on the other hand, is a matter of the interpretation of the Bible, hermeneutics: "The place of women in the Bible is an interpretive, hermeneutical question. It is not an inerrancy question."[2]

WHAT IS INERRANCY?

Inerrancy is a somewhat difficult concept, easier to claim and/or defend than to define. People have taken three approaches in dealing with the difficulty posed by the frequently used term.

1. *There are broad, general definitions.* Inerrancy has been called "a metaphor for the determination to trust God's Word completely."[3] That certainly qualifies as a broad, general definition. Thus, inerrancy can be applied to the Bible in the sense of its being an authentic, dependable record of God's self-disclosure. This seems to be what many laypeople mean who use the term. To them "I believe in inerrancy" means "I believe the Bible." Clark Pinnock said this of Bernhard Ramm: "For him inerrancy always meant something quite simple. It signaled one's commitment to trust the Bible and to take it seriously."[4]

2. *There are more specific, detailed definitions.* David Dockery is a Southern Baptist leader with unquestioned conservative credentials. He has a fine basic definition: "The Bible in its original autographs, properly interpreted, will be found to be truthful and faithful in all that it affirms concerning all areas of life, faith, and practice."[5]

This definition is attractive for several reasons. It is a positive statement. It says that the Bible *has* to be properly interpreted. It argues that the Bible is true in what it affirms, in what it teaches, not merely in what it records or reports. Dockery calls this critical inerrancy, not naïve inerrancy (see below).

3. *Still, a more precise, technical definition is sought by many people.* In fact, Dockery himself has a longer and much more involved definition.[6] The most famous such definition is of course that of the Chicago Council on Biblical Inerrancy in 1978.[7] It is certainly not simple. There is a preface, a five-part summary, and then nineteen explanatory or qualifying articles, plus four pages of exposition.

BIBLICAL AUTHORITY AND INERRANCY

On the popular level, then, "inerrancy" seems to indicate a belief in the Bible, acceptance of the Bible, and submission to the authority of the Bible. Some, however, want more. Some people seem to want to retreat into the redoubt of inerrancy in an attempt to ensure that their interpretations of Scripture will be mandatory: *I believe the Bible, and therefore the way I choose to interpret it must obviously be correct.*

When I was a seminary student—back during the "Jurassic Period" of the 1950s—the question then was, "Is the Bible inspired?" When I was a graduate teaching fellow, I had a student ask me, "Do you believe that the Bible is inspired?" That was what counted at that time. That category was sufficient. That was the issue, the question. It was enough.

But it turned out not to be enough. Not everyone who believes that the Bible is inspired comes up with the same interpretations. So some have felt that more strict categories are necessary. The new watchword became *verbal inspiration*, having to do not merely with broad concepts but with words. However, predictably, that too turned out not to be enough. Then, as I remember it, we moved on to *plenary verbal inspiration*.[8] But that was still not enough. Everyone who agreed to the category of plenary verbal inspiration did not come up with the same interpretation, the correct interpretation, in other words, *my* interpretation. Then people began to call the Bible "infallible." There was the same eventual result. So, relatively recently, the category of inerrancy was developed.[9] Now the question is, Do you believe that the Bible is inerrant? Do you believe in inerrancy?

I personally think that this rather long-running struggle has been an attempt to ensure that everyone will interpret the Bible the same way.[10] However, it has not been successful, and it never will be successful. People equally committed to inerrancy will still interpret the Scriptures differently. Here is a relevant example: There are inerrantists who believe in the ordination of women, and there are inerrantists who oppose the ordination of women.[11] The crucial issue is obviously not inerrancy, but interpretation. David Dockery has agreed that "an affirmation of biblical inerrancy does not in itself guarantee orthodoxy."[12]

Here is another example of the distinction between inerrancy and interpretation. One of the founding fathers of the doctrine of inerrancy was B. B. Warfield of Princeton Seminary. He has been correctly called "a champion of biblical authority and inerrancy."[13] However, Warfield said that inerrancy is "not essential to Christianity. It is not the essence of Christianity."[14] Warfield was a postmillennialist—an inerrantist, but a postmillennialist. He also believed in theistic evolution. This is the "champion of biblical authority and inerrancy." The fact that he believed in inerrancy had a lot to do with what he believed about the Bible, but not a lot to do with how he interpreted and applied it. People equally committed to inerrancy will still interpret the Scriptures differently.

VARIETIES OF INERRANCY

I once heard Gabriel Fackre name three different types of inerrantists. David Dockery, on the other hand, has identified nine different types.[15] They represent different views on what it means to say that the Bible is trustworthy and authoritative. Dockery has given examples of each type.[16]

1. *Naïve inerrancy* (mechanical dictation). In this view, God actually dictated the Bible to the human writers. There was "little or no involvement of the human writers in the process."[17] According to this view, there are passages that indicate the Spirit of God told the author precisely what to write; these "are regarded as typical of the entire Bible. The strength of this position is that it gives proper credit to God as the author of the Bible. However, it seemingly ignores style differences, as well as historical and cultural contexts."[18]

2. *Absolute inerrancy.* This position "allows for more human involvement."[19] The Bible is accurate and true in all matters, and the writers intended to give a considerable amount of data on such matters as history, science, and geography. This view tries to avoid mechanical dictation, but it affirms instead a verbal-plenary view of inspiration instead. It tries to affirm that the Bible is the written word of God but also to account for human authorship. Sometimes, however, this view also seems to fail to take seriously the human aspect of Scripture and its historical contexts.[20]

3. *Critical or balanced inerrancy.*[21] The Bible is true in all that it affirms, to the degree of precision intended by the biblical author. This view does not try to harmonize every detail of Scripture. It realizes that the authors had different purposes—Matthew and Luke, for example, or the authors of Kings and Chronicles. This view uses, cautiously, critical methodologies such as form criticism and redaction criticism. This position usually regards scientific matters as phenomenal—spoken of in popular language that describes things as they appear, without overly precise or technical language. Historical matters are faithful representations of the way the events described took place. However, this was accuracy in general, not precise, terms.[22] This is Dockery's personal position.[23]

4. *Limited inerrancy.*[24] The Bible is inerrant in all matters of salvation and ethics. The old Baptist phrase I grew up on was "matters of faith and practice." Divine inspiration did not raise the writers to an intellectual level above that of their contemporaries. It did not give them scientific knowledge unavailable to the people of their day. Therefore, it is possible that the Bible may contain "errors" of science or history in the sense that it expresses the common understandings of that ancient day.[25] The problem with this view is that it makes the human writer responsible for recent developments in scientific and historical methods. However, the point of the view is that the Bible is fully truthful and inerrant in matters for which it was given.[26]

5. *Qualified inerrancy.* "This position is . . . similar to the one identified above, except in matters of philosophical starting points. The previous

position is more closely identified with empiricism, while this one begins with a strong viewpoint of faith." It is qualified inerrancy in that "inerrancy can be maintained if we qualify it as a faith statement." We are looking through the eyes of faith. "It is possible that errors could be identified through an inductive study, but beginning with the presupposition of faith, a position of inerrancy . . . can be maintained in a 'qualified' sense." This position is obviously somewhat difficult to articulate.[27]

6. *Nuanced inerrancy* (or *focused inerrancy*). This view proposes that "how one understands inerrancy depends on the type of biblical literature under consideration."[28] It is quite acceptable to talk about the Bible as mechanically dictated at certain points like the Ten Commandments, places where human authorship seemingly does not enter in. It is acceptable to talk about verbal inspiration in epistolary or historical literature. In matters where the human author has greater freedom for creativity such as poetry, proverbs, or stories, we must allow for a dynamic inspiration. In other words, one position of inspiration is not adequate to deal with the various types of literature represented in the Bible.[29]

This position takes seriously the human authorship of Scripture. It maintains divine inspiration throughout. However, its obvious difficulty is in correctly identifying the genre that the author uses to communicate the message.[30]

7. *Functional inerrancy.* This popular position "maintains that the Bible inerrantly accomplishes its purpose. It sees the purpose of scripture as one of function." We read the Bible to learn how to be rightly related to the Lord in salvation. We read it to learn how to grow in godliness.[31] One scholar observed that "Jesus never turned to holy scriptures for history or geography but rather for a religious insight into the meaning of life and mission."[32] If I read Augustine correctly—perhaps a big *if*—this was his position.[33] E. Y. Mullins, Southern Baptists' greatest theologian, could perhaps be classified under this category. He spoke of an infallibility of purpose rather than a verbal infallibility (inerrancy).[34] This position generally refuses to relate inerrancy to matters of factuality. The Bible is inerrant in that "it is faithful in revealing God and bringing people into fellowship with him."[35]

I came across an illustration that I think will help clarify this view: Suppose you and I were lost in the wilderness. We have no food, and snow will be coming soon. We stumble into a cabin. While wondering what to do, we notice a faded old map on the table. It is torn and dirty, and part of it seems to be missing, but it shows a path from the cabin to a main road where we could find help. You ask, "I wonder if this map is correct? Will it lead us to safety?" We will not know until we follow it. As we follow the map, we discover that indeed it does bring us to safety and help. We know that whether it is faded or full of holes, it is reliable because it has led us and others to safety. The Bible has been that kind of map for many people for centuries. It does not have to be a perfect map to guide us in our spiritual pilgrimage.

Does one variation affect the whole? A small difference between one book and another does not change the central truth being proclaimed. To change the author of one of the biblical books, or to discover mistakes in quotations, chronology, history, or the scientific view of the writer does not affect the fundamental theological truths they are addressing.[36]

8. *Errant yet authoritative.* Inerrancy is irrelevant. This view neither affirms nor denies a position. It rather considers the whole argument irrelevant, distracting, and concerned with theological minutia that inhibits serious biblical research. This view charges that the debate creates disunity among those who have the main things in common. The major charge against this view is that it fails to see that issues relating to the nature of the Bible and biblical authority are foundational in our faith.[37]

9. *Biblical authority.* This last view does not see the Bible as inerrant, nor as a revelation from God. Rather, the Bible "is a pointer to a personal encounter with God. Questions of truth or falsity are of little concern." This view assumes that the Bible contains errors because it was written by sinful humans. But "the presence of errors in no way militates against the functional purpose or authority of the Bible when God is encountered through reading it." This view obviously has been influenced by Neo-Orthodoxy. It includes an existential or encounter view of truth. It obviously recognizes the situation of the human author, but it does not recognize the divine character of the Scriptures.[38]

Dockery concluded his helpful article by suggesting that we can learn from several, if not all, of these positions. The late Fuller president David Allan Hubbard went much further in stating the obvious: "To recruit students or rally support or withhold fellowship over a definition of biblical inerrancy or the appropriateness of using the term seems futile, if not wicked."[39]

BIBLICAL INTERPRETATION AND FEMALE EQUALITY

Hermeneutics, on the other hand, involves the principles by which we understand and apply the Bible, whichever one of the many doctrinal positions about the nature of the Bible we may hold. The principles and practice of interpretation are the same, whatever doctrinal stance one may take. Here, of course, is where equality arises. Egalitarianism is the conviction that, when taken as a whole and when properly interpreted, the Bible teaches the equality of female and male in the world, the church, and the home.

Does not Galatians 3:28 state a universal theological principle, "there is no longer male and female," while 1 Timothy 2:12, "I permit no woman to teach or to have authority over a man; she is to keep silent," is an accommodating response to a specific congregational problem? The answer is one of hermeneutics, not inerrancy.

Does not Genesis 1:28 ("God blessed *them*, and God said to *them*, . . . 'have dominion'") lay down a basic principle of equality, in light of which any subsequent passages seeming to give woman a subordinate place need to be understood? The answer is one of hermeneutics, not inerrancy.

Does not Ephesians 5:21, "Be subject to one another," dictate that the statements that follow must be seen in light of mutual submission? Again, it is hermeneutics, not inerrancy. The two are different though related matters.

Yes, it is possible to believe in biblical authority, inerrancy, and female equality—and I do. ✛

NOTES

[1] Miller McClure, "Then get out," *Baptist Standard* 111/47 (1 December 1999): 4.

[2] Gary Burge, quoted in "Submission Rejected," *Christianity Today* (6 December 1999): 27.

[3] Clark H. Pinnock, *The Scripture Principle* (San Francisco: Harper and Row, 1985), 225.

[4] ———, "Bernard Ramm: Postfundamentalist Coming to Terms with Modernity," *Perspectives in Religious Studies* 17/4 (Winter 1990): 24.

[5] David Dockery, "Can Baptists Affirm the Reliability and Authority of the Bible?" *SBC Today* (March 1985): 16.

[6] "When all the facts are known, the Bible (in its autographs) properly interpreted in light of which culture and communication means had developed by the time of its composition will be known to be completely true (and therefore not false) in all that it affirms, to the decree of precision intended by the author, in all matters relating to God and his creation (including history, geography, science, and other disciplines addressed in Scripture)." Quoted by Wayne Ward, review of *Authority and Interpretation: A Baptist Perspective*, eds.

Duane A. Garrett and Richard R. Melick Jr. in *Criswell Theological Review* 3/1 (Fall 1988): 226.

[7] "The Chicago Statement on Biblical Inerrancy," *The Journal of the Evangelical Theological Society* 21/4 (December 1978): 289-96.

[8] "Plenary" means "fully, thoroughly, completely." A plenary session is a session where everyone attends. This is the view that every word is fully (hence "plenary") inspired, so therefore the whole Bible is inspired.

[9] "The term has been used sparingly in Protestant circles until the present time" (William L. Hendricks, in personal conversation [4 February 2000]).

[10] It is an attempt at "'nailing down' a concept of religious authority that cannot be challenged or evaded" (W. R. Estep, unpublished paper, "The Nature and Use of the Bible in Baptist Confessions of Faith," 1).

[11] See Gilbert Bilezikian, *Beyond Sex Roles: A Guide for the Study of Female Roles in the Bible* (Grand Rapids: Baker Book House, 1985); and James Hurley, *Man and Woman in Biblical Perspective* (Grand Rapids: Zondervan Publishing Company, 1981).

[12] Dockery, "Can Baptists Affirm the Reliability and Authority of the Bible?" 16.

[13] James T. Draper, *Authority: The Critical Issue for Southern Baptists* (Old Tappan NJ: Revell, 1984), 65.

[14] Clark H. Pinnock, "What is Evangelicalism?" cassette TC 5872, Southwestern Baptist Theological Seminary library, Fort Worth TX.

[15] David Dockery, "Variations on Inerrancy," *SBC Today* (May 1986): 10-11.

[16] In a student forum at Southwestern Seminary on 23 January 1991, Dockery identified the absolute and critical categories with the Chicago statement, articles 12 and 13.

[17] William H. Stephens, "Inerrancy: more than just a preacher's battle," *Baptist Standard* (19 February 1992): 16.

[18] Dockery, "Variations," 10.

[19] Stephens, "Inerrancy," 16.

[20] For example, Harold Lindsell, *The Battle for the Bible* (Grand Rapids: Zondervan Publishing House, 1976).

[21] In a student forum at Southwestern Seminary, Dockery said that the critical and limited expressions wrestle with the problem of the divine-human authorship of Scripture.

[22] For example, Roger Nicole and J. Ramsey Michaels, *Inerrancy and Common Sense* (Grand Rapids: Baker Book House, 1980); D. A. Carson and John Woodbridge, *Scripture and Truth* (Grand Rapids: Zondervan Publishing House, 1983).

[23] Stan Norman, "Dr. David S. Dockery," *The Student Forum* 9/2 (January 1991): 2.

[24] In the student forum, Dockery associated this position with E. Y. Mullins.

[25] We do exactly the same thing: We say that the sun rose (wrong!), we say that the sun did not shine all day (error!), we talk about heavy clouds, and we still speak of the four corners of the earth—all wrong but still commonly expressed. On the question of defining "error" in Scripture, see David Hubbard, "The Current Tensions: Is There a Way Out?" in *Biblical Authority*, ed. Jack Rogers (Waco TX: Word Books, Publisher, 1977), 168. This is an excellent article and is highly recommended.

[26] For example, I. Howard Marshall, *Biblical Inspiration* (Grand Rapids: William B. Eerdmans Publishing Company, 1982).

[27] Dockery, "Variations," 10. For example, Donald Bloesch, *Essentials of Evangelical Theology*, I (San Francisco: Harper and Row, 1979).

[28] Grant Lovejoy and Steve Lemke, *A Manual for Biblical Hermeneutics* (Fort Worth: Southwestern Baptist Theological Seminary, 1993), 21.

[29] Dockery, "Variations," 10.

[30] For example, Pinnock, *The Scripture Principle*, and perhaps also Donald Bloesch, according to a review by David Dockery, *Criswell Theological Review* 1/2 (Spring 1987): 441.

[31] Dockery, "Variations," 10. Also Hendricks: "Biblical inerrancy means that the Bible is adequate to do what it claims in itself that it is intended to do" (personal conversation).

[32] Carroll Stuhlmueller, *New Paths through the Old Testament* (New York: Paulist Press, 1989), 87.

[33] Jack Rogers, *The Door Interviews*, ed. Mike Yackonelli (Grand Rapids: Zondervan Publishing Company, 1989), 172-73.

[34] W. Boyd Hunt, "Southern Baptists and Systematic Theology," *Southwestern Journal of Theology* 1/2 (April 1959): 47 (see also p. 46). Dockery, however, associates Mullins with the limited view.

[35] Dockery, "Variations," 10. For example, G. C. Berkouwer, *Holy Scripture* (Grand Rapids: William B. Eerdmans Publishing Company, 1975); Jack Rogers and Donald McKim, *The Authority and Interpretation of the Bible* (San Francisco: Harper and Row, 1979); Ray Summers, "How God Said It—Part II," *Baptist Standard* (4 February 1970): 12-13. Perhaps also Pinnock and Bloesch; see Dockery review.

[36] William Powell Tuck, "Was Jesus an Inerrantist?" *SBC Today* (March 1985): 18.

[37] Hubbard, "The Current Tensions," 151-81.

[38] Dockery, "Variations," 11. For example, William Countryman, *Biblical Authority or Biblical Tyranny?* (Philadelphia: Fortress Press, 1982).

[39] Hubbard, "The Current Tensions," 178.

CHAPTER SIX

Women Leaders in the Bible
Disobedient Daughters or Models of Ministry?

Audra E. Trull

To write about women leaders in the Bible seems a little like clearing mine fields in Bosnia. Good intentions do not diffuse the dangers. Wherever I step, something or somebody is likely to explode.

Some readers will agree with Simone de Beauvoir, who in *Le deuxieme sexe* claimed that Christian ideology has contributed to the oppression of women.[1] Many post-Christian feminists believe Christianity is irredeemably patriarchal. They have concluded the Bible is one of the primary tools of female oppression and have discarded it as a source of authority, direction, or comfort.

At the other extreme are Christian traditionalists, who are upset by such a disposal of the Scriptures. For them, to discuss the Bible's patriarchal setting or its cultural accommodations is to question its authority—at best it is nonsense, and at worse it is outright heresy. To accept the biblical picture of women's roles is fundamental to their faith in the Bible, so these conventional biblicists say.

A third group, and one growing in numbers and influence, is composed of biblical egalitarians. Sometimes called evangelical feminists,[2] these egalitarians do not believe that the Bible is misogynist, but they challenge some of the ways in which it has been interpreted. By means of careful exegesis and consideration of the cultural context, biblical feminists attempt to uncover the truth about gender relations in Scripture.

The present debate about female equality includes all three opinions. Particularly for Baptists, gender issues have become a matter of major concern.[3] Should women assume roles of leadership in the church, such as teachers, deacons, or even ministers? Church leaders are asking these questions, and more. Since Baptists look to the Bible for guidance, a clear understanding of the teaching of the Scriptures about female roles is needed to respond to these concerns. Those who support a traditional view of women's roles note that the Scriptures portray very few women as leaders. The proper place for women in the Bible is at home; their main role is domestic—wife, mother, and homemaker. This proves, traditionalists believe, that God intended for men to be the leaders.

Christians who support female equality contend that the Bible must be interpreted in light of its cultural and social ethos. Male domination and female subordination are evidence of the fall and not of God's intentional design. Our task today is to restore the pattern of Eden.

The subject of women leaders in the Bible is a key part of this ongoing debate. Biblical egalitarians must begin by explaining the obvious—the fact that very few women appear as leaders in either the Old or the New Testaments. The Bible seems to be mainly about men. Especially when the subject is religious or political leadership, men are the prophets, the priests, the kings, and the overseers of the early church. Yet, a closer look at the Scriptures reveals an amazing paradox. In both the Old and New Testaments, a number of women appear in roles normally reserved for men. These unique female leaders are portrayed as judges, prophets, priests, military leaders, business entrepreneurs, and interpreters of God's will. After the resurrection, women stepped forward to assume the roles of public witnesses, proclaimers of the gospel, called apostles, church deacons, and teachers of men and women.

Are the women leaders in the Bible, few as they may be, simply examples of disobedient daughters, defying the restrictive roles of their day and thereby opposing God's plan for leadership? Or, in light of the cultural and social restrictions of their era, do these examples offer glimpses of God's original intent for females? Could it be that the roles biblical societies and cultures imposed on women reveal sinful oppression by males, not God's order of creation?

I believe the biblical witness is compelling. It is my contention that from the beginning of human history, God intended women to be religious, political, and social leaders. In spite of culturally imposed restrictions, women like Miriam and Mary of Magdala, Deborah and Huldah, and Phoebe and Priscilla occupied positions of leadership in the nation of Israel and in early Christianity.

THE STATUS OF WOMEN IN THE ANCIENT WORLD

The Greek myth of Amazon female warriors who ruled a society in Scythia is pure fantasy. Also idealistic was Plato's just state composed of three social classes of equal people. The reality is that in every society, including Plato's Greek state, women have been treated as second-class citizens.[4]

The basic premise of this chapter is that God created male and female equal in the beginning, but human sin brought oppression and subjugation to women. Thus it is important to know how female subordination developed and how this pattern influenced biblical communities. A look at the roles of women in societies surrounding the Hebrews will help us understand the accepted subjugation of women in the Old Testament.

Of necessity this discussion will be general. It is an attempt to give the lay of the land as a background for the period, without drawing a detailed map. A brief look at the status of women in Assyria and Babylon will provide a glimpse of daily life for women who lived in these cultures.

In contrast to the modern family unit in the Western world, people in ancient Near Eastern society were seen as members of groups rather than as individuals. The patriarch was both spokesman and representative, making decisions about business arrangements, marriages, and legal matters for the whole group; women were viewed as property, companions, and clan members.

In matters of marriage, divorce, and widowhood, Babylonian and Assyrian women were legally subordinate to their fathers and to their husbands. Adultery was considered an offense against the husband's property and a violation of the husband's rights. Women were restricted to the home, although sometimes allowed to participate in social and commercial activities.

The early rise of goddess worship and a female kinship system were closely entwined in the ancient Near East. There was a gradual shift from a matriarchal system, influenced by the patriarchal invaders around 2400 BC. The social and religious history of the area became increasingly male-oriented.

WOMEN IN HEBREW CULTURE

The images of women in Hebrew society have much in common with what we know of the lives of females in the ancient Near East. The traditional view of historians is that the woman's "place" in Jewish life was maternal and domestic. Joachim Jeremias describes the great control Hebrew men had over women in that day with the phrase *patria potestas*—"fatherly power."

Where did these ideas of male superiority and female subordination come from? Did the practices of Israel's neighbors exert a significant influence upon their gender relations, as it did on their religion? Since the Old Testament reflects a patriarchal society, when and how did the practice of male dominance and female subjection begin? These questions may be impossible to answer, but we do know that this patriarchy was not God's plan in the beginning.

Creation of Humanity. The opening chapters of the Bible give the story of creation and God's pattern for human life. For example, God's unitive purpose for marriage is revealed in Genesis 2:24: "Therefore, a man leaves his father and his mother and clings to his wife, and they become one flesh." Likewise, the first two chapters of Genesis record the story of the creation of humanity as male and female and the meaning of our sexuality. On the surface, the first narrative appears to present woman equal with man (1:24-30); the second seems to subordinate woman to man (2:7-25). A closer look is needed.

The opening chapter of Genesis stresses that both sexes were created simultaneously in the very image of God: "Let us make humankind in our image, according to our likeness; . . . in the image of God he created them; male and female he created them" (Gen 1:26-27). Some argue with Augustine that the woman *with* her husband is the image of God, but she alone is not.[5] However, this passage clearly affirms that both male and female equally share God's image. In addition, the first man and woman are equally responsible to God as stewards of the created order: "Let them have dominion" (1:26b). This responsibility is reemphasized in Genesis 2:15 when *adam* is put in the Garden of Eden "to till and keep it."

In the second account of creation (2:4-24), God first formed "man [*ha adam*] from the dust of the ground, and breathed into his nostrils the breath of life; and the man [*ha adam*] became a living being" (2:7). Hebrew language authorities point out that the use of the definite article *ha* before *adam* usually indicates the more inclusive idea of "humanity" (as in Gen 3:24), which the NRSV translation reflects.[6]

Many biblical scholars argue that the Hebrew *adam* (related to *adamah*, "earth") could be more accurately translated "earth creature," a human being originally without gender.[7] This point is supported by Fuller Seminary theologian Paul Jewett, who contends, "Not only do men and women alike participate in the divine image, but their fellowship as male and female is what it means to be in the image of God . . . . To be Man [*adam*] is to be male or female, male and female, . . . To talk about Man [*adam*] as such is precisely to talk about Man as man and woman."[8]

In this second story of creation, the "earth creature" (*adam*) was separated into male (*ish*) and female (*ishshah*) in Genesis 2:22. Out of the undifferentiated humanity of *adam*, male and female emerged, and Adam cried, "This is bone of my bones and flesh of my flesh" (2:23). Adam awoke from his sleep to see a reflection of himself, a complement to himself, indeed a very part of himself.

Another verse in this second chapter often quoted to support some form of female differentiation is the depiction of the wife as a "helper" ("help meet," v. 18 KJV). Reflecting on this verse, one traditionalist wrote,

> So, was Eve Adam's equal? Yes and no. She was his spiritual equal, and, unlike the animals, 'suitable for him,' but she was not his equal in that she was his 'helper.' . . . A man, just by virtue of his manhood, is called to lead for God. A woman, just by virtue of her womanhood, is called to help for God . . . . It is the word 'helper' that suggests the woman's supportive role.[9]

Does this term connote a secondary position? The word translated "helper" is the Hebrew word *ezer* used fourteen of twenty-one times to refer to God as a superior helper (Exod 18:4). Along with the next word in the verse, "alongside" (*neged*), the two words are sometimes translated "a power equal to him." To argue that the word "helper" connotes an inferior or subordinate role is neither biblical nor consistent with the usage of these Hebrew terms.[10]

Thus the two creation narratives are not contradictory, but rather present a consistent view of maleness and femaleness. From the beginning both sexes were created in God's image and, as such, were equally responsible to God.

However, something disastrous happened in the next chapter of human history—sin and evil became a part of the human condition (Gen 3). The results for male and female relationships were ruinous. One statement found there is often quoted to support male headship in marriage: "Yet your desire shall be for your husband, and he shall rule over you" (3:16). Conservative biblical scholars agree, almost without exception, that this was not intended to be a prescriptive command from God. Rather it is a description of how relationships between men and women would be damaged by the work of sin.

Jewish Patriarchy. As predicted, male domination became the order of the day in Jewish culture. Women were quickly relegated to a secondary position in society, sometimes treated more like property than people. For most women, the great events of their lives were birth, marriage, giving birth, and death.

The Israelite family pattern was centered on the tribe or clan, members tracing their relationships back through their patriarchal fathers to Abraham. Hebrew family life preserved the leadership and the authority of the husband at every turn. Inheritance was passed on through the males and genealogies mainly recorded male family members.

Given such a framework, it should not be surprising that this power was often misused. The father was generally the one who arranged marriages, and sometimes he sold daughters into slavery in order to pay off debts. Men had as many wives and concubines as they could support, and both cultic and secular prostitution was common. Israel's laws did provide some protection from abusive males for wives and children (Deut 22:13-29), yet in matters of divorce and sexual offenses, the male was in control and the woman was severely punished for misdeeds allowed to men (Deut 24:1-4).

Social life involved many restrictions. Although some women were allowed to be shopkeepers in the marketplace, and many could move about in public, a female was not to talk seriously or at length with a man in public or in private. Few women held public office.

In the religious realm, women could not serve as priests, could offer no sacrifices, and were not allowed in certain areas of the temple grounds. They could not enter the Holy Place or the court of men, and they could only use certain gates. A Hebrew woman could participate in some of the religious festivals, but she was not required to attend the Passover, Pentecost, or the Feast of the Tabernacles as were the men. Women could not be instructed in the law. Even the synagogues (which emerged during the Babylonian Exile) contained separate galleries for women.

Like its surrounding culture, Israel reflected a thoroughly patriarchal culture. Male authority in marriage, legal responsibility in civil matters, and leadership in religious functions are uniformly witnessed from the day of Abraham to the time of Jesus.

WOMEN LEADERS IN THE OLD TESTAMENT

Given the male-oriented society prevalent in the Israelite community, it is indeed amazing to find any evidence of women occupying leadership positions in the Old Testament. Yet we cannot ignore the stories of women leaders who served as judges, military leaders, business managers, prophets, and even one who served as a priest in a time of crisis (Exod 4:25-26).

Although a number of Hebrew women could be discussed, I have chosen to highlight the stories of four representative female leaders from Israel's history. To understand the roles they occupied and how they were called to be leaders is to answer the question posed by the title of this chapter.

Miriam. One of the earliest women leaders in Israel's history is Miriam. She first appears as the sister of Moses, watching over her infant brother, who is in a basket among the reeds along the Nile. Jochebed, their mother, hid the infant there to protect him after Pharaoh decreed all male Hebrew babies should die. When Pharaoh's daughter discovered the child, it was Miriam who suggested a "nurse" for Moses—none other than their mother, who nursed Moses until the Egyptian princess took him as her own son (Exod 2:1-10).

Miriam next appears immediately after the Israelites, fleeing from Egypt, have crossed the Red Sea on dry land by divine deliverance. Designated here as a prophet ("one who speaks for God"), she leads the women's chorus in a celebration of the exodus by composing and singing a psalm of praise to God (Exod 15:20-21).

Miriam's awareness of God's call to be a prophet appears in a strange way. She and her brother Aaron were upset with Moses because he married a Cushite woman. The two of them spoke as one, saying, "Has the LORD spoken only through Moses? Has he not spoken through us also?" (Num 12:1-2).

What follows is an unexpected affirmation of Miriam's role as a prophet by Jehovah's rebuke of her resentfulness. The Lord appeared and called the three of them to the tent of meeting, where he reprimanded Miriam and Aaron. Noting his revelations to them and other prophets in visions and dreams, he reminded the two of his special relationship to Moses "face to face" (Num 12:4-10).

From the closing pages of the Old Testament, the prophet Micah praises Miriam as a spiritual leader, along with Moses and Aaron (Mic 6:4). Can there be any doubt that God set apart Miriam to be one of Jehovah's earliest prophets?

> By definition, prophetic activities ascribed to women should not
> be different from those attributed to their male counterparts . . . .
> The common denominator for all these activities is that they are

understood to spring from a direct and legitimately claimed divine inspiration. This inspiration is bestowed upon the prophet even against his wishes, and he has no choice but to accept the divine mission.[11]

Deborah. Among the women leaders in the Old Testament, Deborah embodies more major roles of leadership than most men in Israel's history. She certainly lived up to her name, which means "a bee"—she was busy, intelligent, and gave a fatal sting to her enemies the Caananites. Like Miriam, she was a prophet and spiritual leader who spoke for God to the Hebrew people. In addition, Deborah was "judging Israel at that time" (Judg 4:4), serving as the highest public official of that day. Handpicked by God to administer justice in the land (Judg 2:16), she became one of the strongest judges in Israel's history.

As the supreme political leader, Deborah was also the ultimate authority in time of war. She was specifically chosen to deliver Israel from the oppressive regime of the Canaanites and the army of Sisera. As a military leader, Deborah adopted a plan, organized troops, and went about to destroy the enemy. At the Israelite commander Barak's request, she led the Hebrew army to victory (Judg 4:6-16). Another female, Jael, completed the mission in an unwomanly way—she drove a peg through fleeing Sisera's head while he was sleeping (Judg 4:21).

After her victory over the Canaanites, Deborah composed a song that is regarded as one of the finest specimens of ancient Hebrew poetry, rivaling even the celebrated song of Miriam.

Thus, as the fifth judge of Israel, Deborah fulfilled several roles: she served as a prophet, administered justice, led the Israeli army to victory, and composed a praise song to God. Her greatest contribution was that she led the people back to God, arousing the nation from its lethargy and despair. "Hers was a fearless and unsolicited devotion to the emancipation of God's people, and she awoke in them a determination to free themselves from their wretched bondage and degradation."[12]

During the decades of peaceful existence that followed the victory over the Canaanites, Deborah continued to bring justice throughout the nation of Israel, "and the land had rest forty years" (Judg 5:31).

Huldah. Though not a well-known personality, Huldah appears as an important actor in one of the most familiar stories in the Old Testament—the discovery of the Book of the Law during Josiah's reign from 640 to 609 BC (2 Kgs 22:8-20 and 2 Chr 34:14-34). As a prophet in Jerusalem, Huldah could be found sitting in the central part of the city, ready to receive and counsel any who wished to inquire of Jehovah.

When the priest Hilkiah found a book during the repair of the temple, the scroll was taken and read to young King Josiah. Though the exact contents of the book are unknown, most scholars think it was the central section of Deuteronomy (12–26).[13] Josiah was so impressed with the message of this scroll that he sent emissaries to "inquire of the LORD for me, for the people, and for all Judah concerning the words of this book that has been found" (2 Kgs 22:13).

To whom did the priest Hilkiah and his associates turn for divine confirmation? Not to a male theologian or prophet, although Jeremiah and Zephaniah were alive then, but the officials went to a woman prophet, "Huldah, the wife of Shallum" (2 Chr 34:22). The temple prophet Huldah became an interpreter of the word of God for Israel. Huldah was able to relate to the king the destiny of the Jewish nation. Like other true prophets, she delivered a message of judgment against Israel's idolatry and lifestyle, as well as a word of hope for the penitent. Huldah's story is also notable in that she authorizes what will become the core of Scripture for Judaism and Christianity.[14]

The fact that King Josiah and the High Priest of Judah believed that Huldah was the one to interpret the word of God at this crisis point in Judah's history establishes her role as a woman leader. The female prophet's word was accepted by all of Israel as a divinely revealed message. "In that male-dominated, thoroughly patriarchal society, it was a woman that had to interpret Holy Scripture for the King of Judah, the High Priest, and three other men of distinction!"[15] Huldah's message from God, coupled with her identification of the Book of the Law found in the temple, triggered the great revival under King Josiah (2 Kgs 23).

Ideal Woman of Proverbs. Our final example of a woman leader in the Old Testament is the nameless ideal wife described in Proverbs 31:10-31. Every Mother's Day in countless pulpits she is honored as the biblical picture of a perfect woman.

Many believe the portrait is too idealistic. Granted, it is hard to imagine a woman in any culture having the time or strength to fulfill all of these roles in one lifetime! Even the biblical writer notes that such wives are rare (31:10). It is probably a mistake to assume that all the virtues in this description are likely to be embodied in one woman. The poetic structure of this eulogy supports the view that the writer has not a single individual in mind, but a composite picture of a capable wife.

There is no doubt, however, that this passage was meant to extol the virtues of a good wife and mother. The range and excellence of her household talents are expected. What does surprise the reader is this: intertwined with her many domestic qualities are numerous enterprises that are normally reserved for men. Notice how this model Hebrew woman assumes male roles, engaging in various business activities outside her home. As a commercial entrepreneur, she profits from her merchandise (v. 18), selling garments and sashes (v. 24); as a realtor, she appraises land and buys it (v. 16a); and as a farmer, she plants and oversees her own vineyard (v. 16b).

If indeed this inspired picture is the supreme expression of ideal womanhood in the Hebrew Scriptures, then her participation in commercial ventures outside the home is important. They remind the patriarchal males of Hebrew society that God did not intend women to be limited to domestic duties, living in seclusion.

The inspired writer of Proverbs gave a complete picture of the total woman from God's point of view.

> Suffice it to say that the wife shares in her husband's dignity and must never be reduced to a position of chattel or slave. Proverbs 31:10-31 celebrates that godly wife for her managerial talents and business acumen, for being a gracious mother and wife, and for having authority and a clear sense of personal worth. Any reduction of the status of women is a result of sin.[16]

WOMEN IN THE NEW TESTAMENT WORLD

The writings of Philo and Josephus provide samples of Jewish attitudes toward women in general at the time of Christ. Philo explained the difference between males and females: men are informed by reason (*nous*), women by sensuality (*aisthesis*).[17] Josephus is more blunt: "the woman is inferior (*cheiron*) to the man in every way."[18]

Although Jewish women occupied a position of dignity and responsibility in the home, in social life they continued to be little more than an appendage of their husband. After describing a woman's official position as very low, William Barclay commented: "In Jewish law she was not a person, but a thing; she was entirely at the disposal of her father or her husband. She was forbidden to learn the law; to instruct a woman in the law was to cast pearls before swine."[19] Jewish women had no part in the synagogue service, could not teach in school, were not obligated to attend sacred feasts, and their testimony was not credible evidence in the courts.

Talking to women in public was strictly forbidden. A rabbi would never greet a woman on the street, not even his own wife or daughter. In the traditional Jewish morning prayer, a man offered thanks that God had not made him "a Gentile, a slave, or a woman."

In the Graeco-Roman world of the first century, the situation was no better. In many ways it was worse. The respectable Greek woman lived a secluded life; confined to her quarters, she normally appeared in public only once or twice each year.

Demosthenes explained the accepted role of the Greek wife: "We have courtesans for sake of pleasure; we have concubines for the sake of daily cohabitation; we have wives for the purpose of having children legitimately, and of having a faithful guardian for all our household affairs."[20] The wife's primary function was to bear a male heir for her husband.

The role of women in religion, both Greek and Roman, was inferior and degrading. Jesus, however, introduced a radical idea. As Jesus and the Twelve traveled from village to village, many women accompanied the group and "provided for them out of their resources" (Luke 8:1-3). By allowing these healed and transformed women to join his missionary band, Jesus was challenging the idea that women were not to be involved in God's work or associated with men in this mission.

Women are prominent players in the opening chapters of Christian history. Among the thousands of females who followed Christ, scores became church leaders, serving as apostles, deacons, teachers, personal witnesses, and interpreters of the Christian way. These women leaders were among the most conspicuous examples of the transforming power of Christianity.

To illustrate and affirm the thesis of this chapter, let us once again examine four prime examples of women who modeled leadership in the New Testament. This quartet adds weight to our contention that women and men are equally endowed by God with leadership gifts.

Mary Magdalene. Mary came from Magdala, a town known for both wealth and immorality. Tradition has it that Mary was herself a scarlet sinner, as wicked as the town of her birth.

Mary first appears with a list of women who had been cured of various diseases. Jesus reclaimed, forgave, and purified her. Mary had sinned much;

73

now she loved much. As Jesus and the Twelve traveled from village to village, Mary joined the group of women who assisted in caring for the disciples' daily needs (Luke 8:2-3). Evidently she stayed near Jesus until the very end. She was at Calvary when Jesus was crucified and, along with other devoted women, was among the last to leave (John 19:25).

As a final act of devotion, Mary of Magdala returned to the sepulcher "early on the first day of the week" (John 20:1) to say her final goodbye to her Lord. It was customary in Palestine to visit the tomb of a loved one three days after burial. In the gray dark, Mary realized the circular stone that sealed the tomb had been removed. She assumed someone had stolen the body, or possibly the stone had been removed by grave robbers. Not knowing what to do, Mary returned to Jerusalem to report the tragic discovery to Peter and John, who raced to investigate.

Not hearing from Peter and John, Mary assumed foul play and retraced her steps. Arriving at the tomb entrance, Mary peered into the sepulcher and saw two figures sitting where Jesus' body had laid. "Why are you crying?" one asked.

Mary then turned around to discover someone standing in the garden, who said, "Woman, why are you weeping? Whom do you seek?" Thinking this was the gardener, she replied, "Sir, if you have carried him away, tell me where you have put him, and I will get him" (John 20:15).

A single word turned her grief into joy: "Mary!" Her reply "Rabboni" was a spontaneous confession. When Mary fell adoringly at the feet of Jesus and grasped him, the risen Christ gently corrected her error. "Do not hold on to me, for I have not yet returned to the Father. Go to my brothers and tell them" (John 20:17).

Mary ran to share the news of Jesus' resurrection with his disciples, joyously exclaiming, "I have seen the Lord" (John 20:18).

Putting these facts together, it is indeed amazing that the first person to witness the empty tomb and see the risen Christ was a woman—a woman who had been rescued from a life of open shame. The most momentous news in the history of humanity was entrusted to a previously obscure female who, by first-century standards, was least qualified to proclaim it. Her story was easily called into question because of her illness, her past life, and the fact that the Jewish world of the first century did not trust the testimony of any woman (Luke 24:11).

Yet all four Gospels record that the first witnesses to the empty tomb were females. It is significant that Christ waited until the men had left the tomb before he appeared to Mary and the other women (Matt 28:9-10). This was Jesus' deliberate choice.

Mary's prominent role among the women disciples in the Gospels and the use of her name in noncanonical tradition leads to the assumption that she was a leader who held a position of spiritual authority among many Christians.[21]

Priscilla. Through the missionary labors of Paul and his companions, Christianity spread throughout Asia Minor. One of the early women leaders associated with Paul's ministry is Prisca, also referred to by the diminutive form Priscilla. We meet her first in Corinth (Acts 18:2), along with her husband Aquila, where they have recently arrived from Rome because of the expulsion of Jews by the Emperor Claudius.

Aquila and Priscilla had much in common with the apostle Paul. Like him they were Jews, and like him they were tentmakers. The trade they had in common seems to have brought them together. While in Corinth Paul lived and worked with them, and they joined him every Sabbath as he testified before Jews and Greeks (Acts 18:3-4).

After a lengthy stay, Paul left Corinth for Ephesus, accompanied by Priscilla and Aquila (Acts 18:18). Upon reaching Ephesus, Paul left the couple there, pledging to return later. Some suggest that Paul put them in charge of the house church they started.

Interesting in this account is the way the couple is listed. Pricilla is mentioned before her husband not only here, but in four of the six citations of this couple. First-century practice normally mentioned the husband's name only; when the wife's name was listed, it normally came after the man's. The most obvious reason for Prisca's priority would be that she was the stronger of the two or of higher status, though one scholar suggests that probably "she was more important for the Christian community—whether by virtue of nobility, personality, or spirituality is unclear."[22]

What happens next provides a key insight about Priscilla as a woman leader in the early Christian community. An Alexandrian Jew named Apollos arrived in Corinth. An eloquent and enthusiastic speaker, he began teaching about Jesus. But his instruction in the "Way of the Lord" was deficient, as he knew only the baptism of John (Acts 18:24-25). When Prisca and Aquila heard Apollos, they gently took him aside and "explained the Way of God to him more accurately" (Acts 18:26).

The verb used here to describe Prisca's teaching of Apollos is elsewhere used of the public proclamation of the gospel by Peter (Acts 11:4) and Paul

(Acts 28:23). Priscilla's role in teaching Apollos is a strong argument in favor of her role as a church leader and teacher on a par with, if not superior to, her husband. Frank and Evelyn Stagg conclude, "There is no hint here or elsewhere in Acts that a woman should be subordinate, be silent, and not teach a man."[23]

Phoebe. "I commend to you our sister Phoebe, a deacon of the church at Cenchreae, . . . a benefactor of many and of myself as well" (Rom 16:1-2). In two brief verses, Paul commends Phoebe to the Christians at Rome, giving just enough information to affirm her significant role in the early church.

The apostle doesn't explain why Phoebe is in Rome. Some have speculated that she was traveling for business reasons and had agreed to carry this letter as a favor to Paul. Others, however, contend the travel and Paul's recommendation reflect Phoebe's role as a church leader (cf. 1 Cor 4:17, 2 Cor 3:1, Acts 18:27). In addition, the apostle introduces Phoebe as "our sister," suggesting that she, like Timothy, was a coworker, and like Epaphroditus, probably was the one who carried the letter from Paul to the church in Rome.[24]

Phoebe is also identified as a *diakonos* of the church of Cenchreae, the eastern port of Corinth. Sometimes *diakonos* is translated as "servant" (NIV) or "deaconess" (RSV, NJB) and is defined as service in a limited ministry to women or to the sick. However, *diakonos* is the same title (with no gender distinctions) that Paul applies to himself and to others (twenty-one times) for people engaged in their ministry of preaching and teaching (1 Cor 3:5; 2 Cor 6:4; Phil 1:1). "The word clearly points to a leadership role over the whole church not just part of it; and the way the title is introduced suggests a recognized office, . . . a church official, a minister of the church in Cenchreae."[25]

Phoebe is also described as a *prostatis* "of many and of myself as well" (16:2). The feminine form of this noun can denote a position of leadership. In its eight occurrences in the New Testament, the verb consistently means "to stand before, to preside, to rule, to govern"[26] (cf. 1 Thess 5:12). This is the term Paul used to describe the office of deacon (1 Tim 3:8-13) and elder (1 Tim 5:17). Later the established church used the term for civil authorities, ecclesiastical rulers, and bishops.

The emphasis in this passage is on Phoebe's role as benefactor, though the title reinforces the servant-leadership role of church leaders. Evidently Phoebe was a generous benefactor who provided funds for the churches, along with her considerable influence.

For many, Phoebe is the most conclusive evidence in the New Testament that women were in positions of leadership. An independent woman of means, Phoebe is not defined in terms of her husband, father, or family. As Paul's coworker ("sister") and an established church leader ("deacon"), Phoebe may well have been traveling to or through Rome as a missionary, possibly to make preparations for Paul's mission to Spain.

Junia. Not only does Romans 16 confront us with the deacon and church leader Phoebe, but we also meet a lesser-known woman mentioned only here in the Scriptures. During Paul's roll call of the saints in the house churches at Rome, he adds this personal word: "Greet Andronicus and Junia, my relatives who were in prison with me; they are prominent among the apostles, and they were in Christ before I was" (Rom 16:7). In the midst of a long list of people who worked alongside Paul, we meet two fellow-Jews ("relatives") who were believers before Paul and shared in his imprisonment. Their service makes them "outstanding among the apostles" (NASB).

Across the years this verse has raised two textual questions: Is Junia a female and in what sense is Junia an apostle? For our purposes, the first question is basic: Is Junia a woman? Bible translators have rendered the name of this person in both the masculine (Junias, NASB, ASV, NIV) and feminine (Junia, NRSV, KJV) forms. Junia is a common Latin name for a woman, and it is the form found in the biblical (Greek) text. Some have tried to insert "Junias" as a shortened form of Junianus, but Latin diminutives are not formed in this way and the name "Junias" has yet to be found in extra-biblical sources.[27]

In addition, early church leaders Origin, Chrysostom, and Jerome assume that Junia was a woman in their writings. More significant may be the fact that the earliest manuscript of Romans inserts the feminine name "Julia," further proof that a female apostle is acceptable.[28]

Another strategy is to question whether these two were apostles. The phrase "among the apostles," opponents say, only means they were held in high esteem *by* the apostles. However, the preposition used here (*en*) always has the idea of "within."

Craig Kenner summarizes the matter: "Those who favor the view that Junia was not a female apostle do so because of their prior assumption that women could not be apostles, not because of any evidence in the text."[29]

The early church considered it essential that an apostle be a firsthand witness to the resurrection (Acts 1:22). Evidently Junia fulfilled the Pauline criteria for apostleship (1 Cor 9:1) in that she claimed to have seen the risen Christ and had done missionary work. It is possible the Romans imprisoned Junia and Andronicus because of conflicts with the missionary work they did.[30]

Junia, along with Adronicus, apparently helped lay the foundation for the churches at Rome. These "notable apostles" served as Paul's counterpart in that city, preaching, teaching, and ministering. In one brief verse, the biblical text summarized what later Christian tradition affirmed, that Junia was a recognized woman leader in the church.

My conclusion is obvious. In spite of male patriarchy and severe cultural restrictions on females, women leaders rise like majestic mountains in the Bible. Never are they portrayed as disobedient daughters. Rather the roles they occupy are examples of a ministry that is pleasing to God.

Is it any wonder the pagan Libanius exclaimed, "What women these Christians have!" ✝

NOTES

[1] Bonnie Thurston, *Women in the New Testament* (New York: Crossword Publishing Company, 1998), 1.

[2] A leading organization that seeks to educate Christians regarding the equality of men and women is Christians for Biblical Equality, 122 West Franklin Ave., Suite 218, Minneapolis, MN 55404.

[3] See the discussion by the editors in the introduction.

[4] Joe E. Trull, *Walking in the Way: An Introduction to Christian Ethics* (Nashville: Broadman & Holman, 1997), 189. Some material in this section is gleaned from chapter 8.

[5] Ruth A. Tucker, *Women in the Maze* (Downers Grove IL: InterVarsity Press, 1992), 35-36.

[6] Biblical scholar Bruce Metzger notes in the introduction to the NRSV that "in references to men and women, masculine-oriented language should be eliminated as far as this can be done without altering passages that reflect the historical situation of ancient patriarchal culture" (ix).

[7] Morar M. Murray Hayes, "Emancipation of Women," *Encyclopedia of Biblical and Christian Ethics,* ed. R. K. Harrison (Nashville: Thomas Nelson, 1987), 129-31.

[8] Paul K. Jewett, *Man as Male and Female* (Grand Rapids: Eerdmans, 1975), 24.

[9] Raymond C. Ortland Jr., "Male-Female Equality and Male Headship," in *Biblical Manhood and Womanhood* (Wheaton: Crossway Books, 1991), 102, 104.

[10] Tucker, *Women in the Maze,* 37-38.

[11] Athalya Brenner, *The Israelite Woman* (Sheffield, England: JSOT Press, 1985), 57-58.

[12] Herbert Lockyer, *All the Women of the Bible* (Grand Rapids: Zondervan, 1988), 41.

[13] Joe E. Lunceford, "Biblical Women Weren't Always Submissive," in *Pricilla Papers*, Fall 2000, 13.

[14] Claudia V. Camp, "Huldah," in *Women in Scripture* (Grand Rapids: Eerdmans, 2000), 96.

[15] Lunceford, "Biblical Women," 15.

[16] P. R. Gilchrist, "Old Testament Ethics," in *Encyclopedia of Biblical and Christian Ethics*, 292.

[17] Philo, *De Opificio Mundi*, 165.

[18] Josephus, *Contra Apionem*, 2:201.

[19] William Barclay, *The Letters to Timothy, Titus, Philemon* (Philadelphia: Westminster Press, 1975), 66.

[20] ———, *The Letters to the Galatians and Ephesians* (Philadelphia: Westminster Press, 1954), 201.

[21] Carolyn Osiek, "Mary 3," in *Women in Scripture*, 121.

[22] Frank Louis Mauldin, "Priscilla and Aquila," in *Mercer Bible Dictionary*, ed. Watson E. Mills et al. (Macon GA: Mercer University Press, 1990), 712.

[23] Evelyn and Frank Stagg, *Woman in the World of Jesus* (Philadelphia: Westminster Press, 1978), 231.

[24] Jouette Bassler, "Phoebe" in *Women in Scripture*, 135.

[25] Ibid.

[26] G. Abbott-Smith, *Manual Greek Lexicon of the New Testament*, 3rd ed., s.v. *"proistemi."*

[28] Aida Besancon Spencer, *Beyond the Curse* (Nashville: Thomas Nelson, 1985), 101.

[28] Lunceford, "Biblical Women," 16.

[29] Craig S. Keener, *Paul, Women and Wives* (Peabody MA: Hendrickson Publishers, 1992), 242.

[30] Bernadette J. Brooten, "Junia," in *Women in Scripture*, 197.

Jesus and Women

Ruth Ann Foster

"A woman's place." What is that? A woman's place according to
Southern Baptist Convention (SBC) leaders is in the home, in
the nursery, or on the missions field, but never, never in a *man's*
place. Historically the SBC has perpetuated a hierarchical, male-dominated
form of leadership for the church, which they emphatically deny as sexist.
Their belief in the God-ordained subordination of women[1] is rooted in a
faulty interpretation of Genesis 1–3. They fail to recognize that the "apparent" subordination of the woman in Genesis 3:16 resulted from sin.

In no way does women's subordination represent God's original plan for
humanity. Genesis 1:26-28 demonstrates clearly that God created
humankind in the image of God, male and female. The Creator assigned
equal responsibility and dominion over the creation to the man and the
woman. Chapters 1 and 2 of Genesis specify no hierarchy of personhood or
role, but rather designate the complementariness, not superiority or inferiority, of the male and female human beings.

The kingdom established by Jesus restored God's original intent that all
humanity, male and female, should represent God in the world. The Gospel
narratives portray Jesus as counter-culture in regards to the treatment of
women. Christ treated them as equal to men, in clear opposition to the prevailing view of the day. Jesus' affirmation and calling of women refute any
idea of sexism in Jesus' reign; tragically, much Baptist doctrine and practice
have essentially disregarded the place of women in Jesus' mission. However,
Baptists must accept Jesus' example as the ultimate revelation for the place of
women in the church and home.

JESUS' "UPSIDE-DOWN" KINGDOM[2]

First-century Jewish leadership rejected Jesus' kingdom values, finding them violently at odds with their own messianic expectations. Not surprisingly, after centuries of political oppression, Palestinian Jews longed for a military/political king to expel their enemies and to enable them to maintain their socio-religious traditions. Jesus found their traditions wanting and challenged any of their traditions that did not adequately represent God; he made no attempt to be subtle about it either. Nor were the leaders subtle in their responses to him; they conspired to kill him (John 11:49-50).

Jesus initiated a radical reversal of "normal" human values of success, morality, and justice. Some have termed his kingdom an "upside-down" kingdom, the first allusion of which is found in Matthew's genealogy. Unexpectedly, Matthew included four rather odd choices for a Jewish genealogy: four Gentile, or Gentile-related, "sexually suspect"[3] women—Tamar, Rahab, Ruth, and Bathsheba. Their inclusion clearly verified that the Jewish messianic kingdom included outsiders and outcast women, thus showing the fulfillment of God's plan for Israel to be a blessing to all the people of the earth (cf. Gen 12:3).

Mary's song of praise (Luke 1:46-55) discloses Luke's first intimation of the "upside-down kingdom." Her hymn prophetically revealed and perhaps influenced the focus of Jesus' words and ministry—a radical reversal in which the downtrodden and humble will be elevated. Mary was among these outsiders as a poor woman from Galilee, perhaps seen by neighbors as unchaste, having become pregnant before marriage. Women were part of Jesus' mission in his ancestry, in the miraculous pregnancies of Elizabeth and Mary, and in the prophecy of Anna.

The incarnation of Jesus Christ, where God became flesh and tabernacled among his people, revealed conclusively the character of God and his kingdom (John 1:18). Luke 4:16-19 records Jesus' self-proclaimed messianic mission to the outcasts and marginalized, those who in Jesus' day were denied full access to the temple—not only Gentiles, but also the diseased and crippled, eunuchs, the very poor, slaves, and women. Jesus' mission began with those likely seen as expendable by the religious leaders, but seen as crucial to a suffering Savior who came to serve. Thus, let us explore the ways Jesus interacted with and ministered to women, who are examples of the marginalized in society.

Over against the traditional argument that women played no significant part in Jesus' ministry, the Gospels unquestionably accord women considerable significance and an essential place in the emerging church. Jesus plainly revealed his view of the proper place of women through his teachings, miracles, close friendships, and religious conversations with women. Jesus often affirmed women's faith and courage. He challenged the "double-standard" that punished only women for adultery, offering a sinful woman grace and forgiveness (John 8:1-11).

Jesus Christ affirmed women as people who possessed intelligence, value, and theological insight; he never "urged them to be feminine or jeered at them for being female."[4] Jesus did not indicate anything unusual about having religious conversations with women, nor did he treat them in a condescending or denigrating manner.[5] The Gospel writers themselves affirmed women for their support of Jesus—women such as Mary Magdalene, Joanna, Susanna, and others who traveled with Jesus and gave financial aid (Luke 8:1-3). Matthew, Mark, Luke, and John also cited the presence of women at the cross and the tomb, and without question the Gospel writers showed that Jesus selected women as the first recipients of the good news of resurrection and the first proclaimers of it.

SOCIAL AND RELIGIOUS ISSUES CONCERNING FIRST-CENTURY JEWISH WOMEN

Examining the status of Jewish females in the first century confirms how radical was Jesus' treatment of women. Jesus was born into a culture that held women in low esteem and in which women had few rights; rabbis even debated whether or not women reflected the image of God or perhaps even possessed souls.[6] Jesus however refused to demean women in words or actions. "[H]is attitude to women was startlingly new, he was able to mix freely and naturally with women of all sorts, and women followed and ministered to him."[7]

Indeed, Jesus elevated women to a place far above that afforded by the Hebrew culture of his day. A Jewish woman's place, much like that of all ancient Near-Eastern women, was primarily in the home,[8] under the control of the male head of the household. "Up to the age of twelve and a half, a father had absolute power over his daughter,"[9] which at marriage was transferred to her husband.[10] The Jewish public census included neither women, slaves, nor minors (Exod 30:11-16),[11] bestowing higher status to male proselytes and freed slaves than to native-born Israelite women.[12]

No doubt many men valued their wives and treated them kindly, but when women consistently heard derogatory remarks about females, their self-respect must have been lowered. In Jesus' day a good Jewish male would thank God daily that he was born neither a slave, a woman, or a dog (Gentile). A rabbi would avoid speaking to women; they were viewed as "manipulative seducers" who cause men to lust.[13] By his teaching and interactions with women, Jesus obviously disavowed the rabbinical idea that all women were seducers. In fact, the teacher from Nazareth taught that women "are to be recognized as subjects in their own right, as fellow human beings, fellow disciples, and not just the objects of men's desire. Their life and rights are to be recognized as important and not to be endangered by the natural desires of men."[14]

In light of Jewish reverence for the Torah, particularly harsh was the saying that burning the Torah was better than allowing a woman to look upon it.[15] Nonetheless, Jesus' conversations with the Samaritan woman and with Martha revealed that both women knew the Torah and that Jesus believed in their ability to comprehend it. Jesus broke down all barriers— racial, religious, gender, or social—that divided people or prevented them from having full access to the grace of God.

JESUS' SELF-REVELATION TO WOMEN

Social and religious barriers never hindered Jesus from ministering to women and calling them to serve as disciples. Four stories in the Gospels highlight the way Jesus related to women in a world that believed women were inferior to men socially, religiously, and morally.

In the first story, Jesus intentionally traveled through Samaria to converse with a woman who lived on the bottom rung of the social, moral, and religious ladder (John 4:1-30). Jews hated Samaritans for a number of historical and religious reasons. Merely to speak to a Samaritan defiled a Jew from worship. In addition, social rules prohibited men from speaking to women in public. The Talmud described one group of religious leaders as "Black and Blue Pharisees." These religious leaders thought that simply looking on a woman caused men to lust. So, when a woman came into view, these pious ones closed their eyes, often causing them to fall down—thus they were given this descriptive name.

Jesus challenged this false attitude toward women by intentionally meeting this "fallen" Gentile woman, who was morally and spiritually unclean. Jesus patiently talked with her about her needs, not letting the woman's prejudice and sarcasm interfere. Because of her previous experiences with men (five husbands and a live-in partner), the Samaritan woman seemed initially skeptical, mocking Jesus' request for a drink. Gradually she became aware that Jesus knew all about her and really cared about her needs. As they talked about worshiping God, Jesus' words had no "hint of separation of male and female, and no hint of other restrictions on women, as would apply in the Temple worship in Jerusalem."[16]

To a moral outcast, to a religious skeptic, and to a shunned Samaritan woman, Jesus offered hope and a new beginning, revealing himself as the promised Messiah, the Christ. How odd. How unusual. But how like an "upside-down" kingdom. This ostracized woman believed Jesus' words and ran to tell the very men who had shunned her. Many Samaritans came to believe in Jesus because of the witness of this first woman evangelist. At the ascension when Jesus announced to the believers that they were to be witnesses in Samaria (Acts 1:8), the risen Lord knew a nucleus of believers already existed in that region. Because of her encounter with Jesus, this Samaritan woman gained "a new network of social relations."[17]

The second story describes a desperate Syrophoenician woman (Mark 7:24-30); evidently Jesus' disciples saw the Gentile mother as a problem. To them she was noisy and pushy, acting in public like a man. From their perspective she had no right to be among them, much less to speak to them. They hoped Jesus would put her in her place. Once again Jesus was quite comfortable conversing with her "as he would with a man who was his [cultural] equal,"[18] both affirming her and granting her request for healing for her daughter.

A third story relates to my personal experience. I was raised in a conservative Baptist church that was heavily influenced by Landmark theology. Women were not allowed to speak publicly in the congregation, not even to lead in prayer or read a report at business meeting. The primary model for a Christian woman was that of Mary, Martha's sister (Luke 10:38-42). According to my church, Mary was quietly devoted to Jesus, as opposed to Martha's harried activity. Against Martha's desire for help, Jesus affirmed Mary's devotion as the better way.[19] Thus, my church taught that a Christian woman must be quiet and submissive, like Mary.

But was Jesus praising her quietness or was he commending her discipleship? Mary's position before the Teacher was the customary one for a disciple in that culture. So, a better interpretation of Jesus' words is the suggestion that Christ affirmed Mary's right to listen and learn like any of his disciples.[20] Women were not second-class citizens in God's kingdom.

The same event is recalled in John's Gospel (12:1-8) and adds another truth to the story. As Martha's sister, Mary knelt and anointed Jesus' feet, then she wiped them dry with her hair. This act of utter humility magnified her devotion to her Lord. Unbinding one's hair publicly was a serious social "sin" only performed by women of low moral status. Evidently Jesus had liberated Mary so completely from all inhibitions that she felt free to disclose her deepest devotion. No longer was she burdened by the expectations of others.

And what about Martha? Churches would not survive without their Marthas, although Martha's busyness has often been criticized as "spiritually" inadequate. Interestingly, the Johannine account of Martha's conversation with Jesus following Lazarus's death corrects the common misconception that she is spiritually weak (John 11:17-29). John's depiction of Martha as a deeply spiritual woman is revealed particularly in her confession of faith (11:27), which for many is more satisfactory than Peter's confession (John 6:68-69).[21]

Martha in her grief reproved Jesus for not preventing Lazarus's death, while also voicing confidence that God would hear Jesus even then. Neither quietly submissive nor busily distracted, Martha surprisingly engaged Jesus in passionate religious debate, much like Job did with God. Jesus did not reprimand Martha for her rebuke; instead, Christ revealed himself as the "Resurrection and the Life" first to her, a woman.[22]

The final story of Jesus' self-revelation to women focuses on Mary Magdalene. Luke implies that this Mary was apparently a woman of independent means, appearing in a list of women who followed Jesus on his journeys and ministered to him out of their own means (Luke 8:1-3). Mary Magdalene also appears in both Matthew's and Mark's accounts of the crucifixion as one of the few who remained with Jesus until the end. All of the Gospel accounts put her at the head of the list of women, indicating a leadership position in this group. Mary from Magdala was a longtime disciple of Jesus, apparently healed by Jesus of a serious infirmity resulting from demon possession (Luke 8:2). She was definitely counted among the "unclean." Still, Jesus did not find her repugnant; rather, he was moved with compassion for her.

Jesus selected Mary Magdalene to receive his first words following the resurrection (John 20:14-18). With a long list from which to choose, the risen Christ appeared first to her, sending Mary forth to be the first proclaimer of the astounding news that Jesus is alive!

Like Paul and others, Mary was a true apostle, "one who is sent with a message" from the risen Lord to tell the others (John 20:17). Her confession to the disciples, "I have seen the Lord" (John 20:18), is reminiscent of Paul's testimony about his apostleship (1 Cor 9:1). Perhaps the early church father, Hippolytus of Rome, recognized her commission when he called Magdalene "the apostle to the apostles."[23]

What makes her choice even more amazing is the fact that in that day a woman could not testify legally, for a woman's witness was invalid and nonbinding.[24] Some skeptics even have questioned her experience as the hallucinations of a formerly demon-possessed woman, suspect and unreliable.[25] Yet, the fact remains that the resurrected Jesus did appear to a woman whom most would consider an unlikely candidate to be the first witness to the resurrection. Mary of Magdala was a woman who had been forgiven much, who loved much, and who stayed near Jesus to the very end.

JESUS' AFFIRMATION OF WOMEN

The four Gospels contain many episodes in which Jesus affirmed women, especially females whom society considered of little worth. Jesus watched a poor widow give her last cent as a temple offering (Luke 21:1-4), and he commended with highest praise her courage and faith. Likewise, in the parable of the lost coin (Luke 15:8-10), Jesus used a woman's plight to explain God's love and concern for every lost person in the world. Here (and in other places) Jesus depicted God in a female role, which gave subjugated women in Hebrew society a new sense of value.

When Jesus healed the woman who had been crippled for eighteen years (Luke 13:10-17), the Son of God called her a "daughter of Abraham," a designation of special honor. This exalted praise effectively removed her from isolation and acknowledged her "as a legitimate member of the Jewish community."[26]

While Jesus was in Bethany, a woman (whom Luke described as immoral) came to anoint the Master with a costly ointment (Mark 14:3-9). Onlookers protested the act, noting the expensive perfume could be sold and the money given to the needy. When Jesus applauded the woman's act of devotion, he was both acknowledging her recognition of his coming Passion and also announcing that in his kingdom outcasts are welcomed. In fact, "Jesus links the prophetic sign of this nameless woman with the proclamation of the gospel throughout the whole world."[27]

Another woman came to Jesus "who had been suffering from hemorrhages for twelve years" (Mark 5:25), as well as enduring hardships from physicians who took her money but did her no good. Due to her malady, she was considered unclean, barred from worship and essentially from any kind of public gathering (Lev 15:19-30). Thus, cut off from God and the community, she was totally without hope. In desperation, she broke the rules by appearing in public and reaching out to touch the One who offered healing. Jesus broke the rules by speaking to her and allowing her to touch him, without first performing the ritual of cleansing. Jesus issued no rebuke, but blessed her faith, calling her "daughter," thus making her his kinswoman.[28]

These four women, along with many others whom Jesus affirmed, found hope and acceptance not available to them through first-century Judaism— hope for a normal life, inclusion into a family, acceptance by God, and participation in a community of faith. No wonder women were loyal to Jesus; "they were finally treated by him as fellow creatures of God without special restrictions."[29]

The story of Jesus and women in the Gospel narratives gives great hope to women of faith today, who passionately long to serve God within the church of Jesus Christ. The way Jesus treated women is a testimony that cannot be refuted. Jesus treated women the same way he treated men, as people created in God's image with gifts and abilities worthy of service in God's kingdom.

Women were essential to the ministry of Jesus. They traveled with Jesus and the Twelve, even to Jerusalem and to the cross, where they witnessed the death and the resurrection of Christ. The eyewitness accounts women gave of "Jesus' ministry, his death, his burial, and his resurrection" serve as "primary apostolic witnesses for the fundamental data of the early Christian faith."[30] Jesus himself "upbraided [the eleven] for their lack of faith and stubbornness, because they had not believed those who saw him after he had risen" (Mark 16:14).

God's choice for servants throughout biblical and human history often surprises us. But Baptists, who claim to be people of "the Book," should not be amazed that God in Christ chose and used women in a culture that denigrated females. This affirmation of women was not a new strategy, but simply a recognition of the creative intent of God in Genesis 1. Both male and female are created equal in the image of God.

Simon Peter caught this vision on the day of Pentecost (Acts 2:14-21), when he declared that the coming of the Holy Spirit upon both men and *women* signaled the inauguration of the last days, as prophesied in Joel 2:28-32. Peter's sermon confirmed that the indwelling Spirit in all believers meant that women and men would prophesy (preach) the good news of Jesus.

Arise, women of faith. Today, more than ever, Christ needs you. Jesus is calling Baptist women, indeed *all* women, to join his band of disciples and use their gifts to promote the kingdom of God. ✢

NOTES

[1] A resolution on women was passed at the annual meeting of the SBC in Kansas City in June of 1984 followed by the 2000 *Baptist Faith and Message* statement on the submission of women.

[2] Donald B. Kraybill, *The Upside-Down Kingdom* (Scottdale PA: Herald Press, 1978).

[3] This terminology is employed by, among others, Luke Timothy Johnson, *The Writings of the New Testament* (Minneapolis: Fortress Press, 1999), 193.

[4] Dorothy Sayers, *Are Women Human?* (Grand Rapids: Wm. B. Eerdmans Publishing Co., 1971), 46.

[5] Ruth Ann Foster, "Jesus, Women, and the Power of Language," *Folio* (Winter 1995): 6.

[6] A current debate exists concerning the place of women in first-century Judaism that shows some evidence of an emerging status for women; nothing of date compares to Jesus' elevation and inclusion of women. For opposing arguments, see Amy-Jill Levine, "Second Temple Judaism, Jesus, and Women," *Biblical Interpretation* 2 (March 1994): 8-33; and Stuart L. Love, "The Place of Women in Public Settings in Matthew's Gospel: A Sociological Inquiry," in *Biblical Theology Bulletin* 24 (Summer 1994): 52-56.

[7] Mary J. Evans, *Women in the Bible* (Downers Grove IL: InterVarsity Press, 1983), 85.

[8] Philo, *Spec. Laws*, 3:169-71.

[9] Bonnie Thurston, *Women in the New Testament: Questions and Commentary* (New York: Crossroad Publishing, Co., 1998), 14.

[10] Ibid.

[11] Love, "The Place of Women," 54.

[12] Ibid.

[13] Jacob Neusner, *A History of the Mishnaic Law of Women* (Leiden: E. J. Brill, 1980), 12, 15.

[14] Ibid.; cf. Eduard Schweizer, *The Gospel According to Matthew* (London: SPCK, 1975), 120-22; cf. Jesus' teachings on lust and divorce, Matt 5:27-32; 19:3-12.

[15] Apparently some women were allowed to read Torah and to have rather secondary places within Judaism. See Ben Witherington, *Women and the Genesis of Christianity* (Cambridge: Cambridge University Press, 1990), 8-9.

[16] Ibid., 72.

[17] Jerome H. Neyrey, "What's Wrong with this Picture? John 4, Cultural Stereotypes of Women, and Public and Private Space," in *Biblical Theology Bulletin* (Summer 1994): 78.

[18] Joanna Dewey, "Jesus' Healings of Women: Conformity and Non-conformity to Dominant Cultural Values as Clues for Historical Reconstruction," *Biblical Theology Bulletin* 4 (Fall 1994): 125.

[19] According to Rikki E. Watts, "Women in the Gospels and Acts," in *Crux* 35 (June 1999): 27, Martha may have been "also offended because she thinks Mary is behaving like a male, not only invading male space but learning Torah."

[20] Susan T. Foh, *Women and the Word of God: A Response to Biblical Feminism* (n.p.: Presbyterian and Reformed Publishing Co., 1979), 90-92.

[21] Witherington, *Women and the Genesis of Christianity*, 106.

[22] Mary-Elise C. Fletcher, "The Role of Women in the Book of John," *Evangelical Journal* 12 (Spring 1994): 45.

[23] Hippolytus, *De Cantico*, 24-26.

[24] Josephus, *Antiquities*, 4:219.

[25] Ernest Renan, *Vie de Jésus* (Paris: Michel Lévy, 1863), 434-35.

[26] Dewey, "Jesus' Healings of Women," 125.

[27] Elisabeth Schüssler Fiorenza, *Jesus: Miriam's Child, Sophia's Prophet* (New York: Continuum Publishing Co., 1994), 95.

[28] Marla J. Selvidge, *Daughters of Jerusalem* (Scottdale PA: Herald Press, 1987), 38.

[29] Witherington, *Women and the Genesis of Christianity*, 68.

[30] Elisabeth Schüssler Fiorenza, *Discipleship of Equals* (New York: Crossroad Publishing Co., 1993), 84.

CHAPTER EIGHT

Paul: Supporter and Exhorter of Women

Catherine Clark Kroeger

The apostle Paul is often viewed as disparaging of women, and yet it would be hard to find affirmations more strongly supportive than those penned by this same missionary to the Gentiles. It was he who wrote that in Jesus Christ there was neither male nor female, Jew nor Gentile, slave or free (Gal 3:28). It was also he who declared that as woman had issued forth from man, so now man issued forth from woman, that the man was not independent of the woman nor the woman independent from the man (1 Cor 11:11-12). All people indeed are from God.

This interdependence of man upon woman and woman upon man forms a basis for much of Paul's missionary strategy. In the days before his conversion, he had persecuted women equally with men, for he understood the importance of their influence and witness. Women had been the primary witnesses of the birth, crucifixion, burial, and resurrection of Jesus; and the raging Saul of Tarsus had been intent upon suppressing their attestations of a reality he wished to deny. When he became convinced that Jesus was indeed the Christ, the Son of God, his primary understanding of the gospel was composed of the very events that the women had proclaimed. He was destined to carry this news throughout the Mediterranean world, bridging the chasm between Jewish and Gentile thought and practice.

Though called to Macedonia by a vision of a man, Paul found in his initial European audience a group of Gentile women who had gathered to worship the true and living God (Acts 16:9-14). The first convert, Lydia, received Paul and Barnabas into her home and her family. It was there that a house church was formed, one that would receive the apostles when they were released from the Philippian jail. In Philippi Paul had risked his life by healing a slave woman, and in Philippi were two women who had served side by side with him in the work of the gospel (Phil 4:3).

One of his major missionary associates was Priscilla, who is mentioned six times along with her husband, though her name usually appears first. She seems to have taken the primary role in instructing the learned Apollos and in establishing a beachhead for Paul's endeavors at Ephesus (Acts 18:26-28). In Corinth the couple had received the apostle into their home, their business, and their fellowship in Christ. They established in their home a house church (1 Cor 16:19), as they would later do in Rome. In the course of their labors, they had risked their necks for Paul and his ministry (Rom 16:3-4).

In the sixteenth chapter of Paul's letter to the Romans, we read of Junia the apostle (v. 7) and of Phoebe the deacon (v. 1) who had been sent to Rome on the business of the church. Phoebe is described as a *prostatis*, an officer of the church at Cenchrae, and apparently she had been placed in that position by the apostle Paul himself. Even before he reached Rome, Paul had cherished friendships with a number of female Christians whom he commends for their service to Christ. He greets the women in the same manner as the men and uses the same words to describe the ministries of both.

Two women mentioned by Paul, Chloe and Nympha, were apparently leaders of house churches (Col 4:15; 1 Cor 1:11); it was the congregation led by Chloe that had the good sense to notify him when serious difficulties arose among the Christians of Corinth. Paul visited the home of four young women who exercised the gift of prophecy, a ministry that Paul himself defined as communicating to the hearer edification, comfort, and exhortation (1 Cor 14:3). Nevertheless, he urged women to adopt a modest head covering when they did so.

Many of Paul's directives to women may be understood in terms of propriety in a culture that often condemned women's religious activities. While many women seldom left their own homes, Paul encouraged women to attend services, to listen attentively to the word of God, and to participate appropriately. In the fourteenth chapter of 1 Corinthians, Paul addresses the matter of disorderly worship. He insists that "all things be done decently and in order" (v. 40).

But such was not the case in Corinth. Therefore he asks that only one person speak at a time, and that the speech be meaningful. If an individual burst into ecstatic speech, then there must be an interpreter to convey the sense to the hearers. Otherwise the speaker must be silent (1 Cor 14:28). If someone were sharing insights given him or her by God and another also experienced a revelation, then the first must be silent so that the second could share (1 Cor 14:30-31). Thus we see that two different types of individuals are enjoined in particular circumstances to maintain silence.

The same terminology is used for a third type of individual, namely women. They too are to be silent under certain circumstances. What are these circumstances? The beginning of chapter 14 describes a worship service that is badly out of control. Indeed, Paul even asks if a visiting unbeliever might not think the congregants were mad (v. 23)! Clearly the instruction to women must be understood in light of the need for order and intelligible communication, with only one person talking at a time and sense being supplied if necessary. Paul seeks to create an environment in which everyone may profit from what is being said. He has already allowed women to prophesy provided their heads are covered (1 Cor 11:5). When, then, may women speak and when are they to be silent?

When Paul wrote that women are told not to "speak" in the congregational service, we must inquire as to the meaning. The Greek word for speaking (*lalein*) occurs over fifty times in 1 Corinthians 14. Many times in this passage it indicates utterances that cannot be understood. Paul even likens the speaking (*lalein*) of some of the worshipers to the strange speech of barbarians whom no civilized person can understand (1 Cor 14:9, 11). A Greek philosopher of the first and second century AD, Plutarch, noted that animals could not carry on a rational conversation, even though apes can chatter and dogs can bark. "Apes and dogs . . . make an utterance [*lalein*] but do not discourse [*phrazein*]."[1] A contemporary of that era observed that *lalein* differs from *legein* (to tell). *Legein* is the orderly bringing forth of rational thought; but *lalein* is the disorderly bringing out of chance utterance.[2]

Lalein frequently does indicate the process of meaningful communication, but not always. At several points, the New Testament uses the term to imply something other than normal human speech.[3] In classical Greek, the word *lalein* sometimes referred to women's meaningless chatter;[4] to this very day one may observe women busily visiting among themselves while an orthodox Jewish service is in progress.

Kari Malcolm used to tell of the efforts of her missionary mother to silence the gossiping of Chinese women while they sat in church. If one does not understand what is going on, it is easy to start another conversation! Thus Paul asks for the women to involve themselves in the service and desires for them to prophesy (14:1, 5). Indeed, they were exhorted to edify the church (14:12) and were permitted to "prophesy one by one so that all may learn and all may be comforted" (14:30).

James encouraged believers to be swift to listen and slow to *lalein* (1:19). Silence sometimes has the sense of listening to what other people have to say. For instance, after hearing of God's work among the Gentiles, the Christians of Jerusalem "were silent and glorified God, saying that evidently God has given the Gentiles repentance unto life" (Acts 11:18). Apparently one can make theological statements while being silent!

Some have suggested that the problem was the desire of women to question what was going on, to ask for an explanation of the concepts being expressed. Women who had never been exposed to written material may well have had a problem understanding what was being read. In that case, Paul is asking them please to wait until they get home. Since communication between husbands and wives was notoriously lacking in Greek homes, this would make an excellent conversation starter.

Alternatively, the women may have been giving themselves to one of the few activities permitted them in some of the ancient cults: that of raising ceremonial cries.[5] Of this there is abundant testimony in ancient literature, artistic representations, and even inscriptions. In Corinth a plaque has been excavated that is dedicated to the "sacred shouts of women." In some ancient rites, emotion rather than meaning was desired, and a clashing of instruments and hubbub of voices indicated a pious observance. *Clamor* was an accepted religious exercise, and the English form of the word is still used today to indicate confused and noisy vociferation.

Paul seems to have had little use for the jangle of sounding brass and tinkling cymbals, both accoutrements of this kind of worship (1 Cor 13:1). And he asks from womenfolk silence rather than shouting, for the word *lalein* can indicate any kind of vocal exercise, even at the top of one's lungs!

If we understand Paul as asking women to be considerate of others who need to hear the word of God, then we can reconcile the command "be silent" (1 Cor 14:34) with the permission to prophesy implicit in 1 Corinthians 11:5. Women are also asked to "be subject" (*hupotasso*) in verse 34, a word that is also used of the prophets two verses earlier. The spirits of the prophets are to "be subject" to the prophets (1 Cor 14:32), indicating that the prophets were able to exercise self-control and cease prophesying when it was someone else's turn. Women were to demonstrate the same ability in refraining from disruptive noise. Theirs was the task of edifying rather than distracting.

In Paul's counsel to Corinthian women, we also need to understand the importance of feminine attire. A woman's head covering was essential for respectability. Anne Carson declared, "Headgear is crucial to female honor, an index of sexual purity and civilized status."[6] This was true in both Jewish and Greco-Roman society.

Since the word "veil" is not used in the passage about "head coverings" (1 Cor 11:2-16), there is scholarly debate as to whether it concerns a woman's unveiled head or her unbound hair. In point of fact, both were considered dangerous and out of order; both would have exposed the congregation and the woman's family to dishonor. In some Jewish groups, divorce was obligatory if a woman appeared in public without her veil. According to Hebrew law, women suspected of adultery were required to have their head uncovered and hair unbound as they stood before the priest. "After the priest has had the woman stand before the LORD, he shall loosen her hair"(Num 5:18).[7]

In the Jewish tractate Daniel and Susanna (also known as Susanna and the Elders) we read, "Now Susanna was a woman of great beauty and delicate feeling. She was closely veiled, but those scoundrels ordered her to be unveiled so that they might feast their eyes on her beauty. Her family and all who saw her were in tears."[8] The unveiling was a disgrace to her and her family.

But the practice was no more acceptable among the Greeks. Unbound and uncovered hair was worn only by women in wildly ecstatic cults and by prostitutes. The respectable woman was veiled, with her hair properly bound up. Sappho wrote that a woman without a head-binder suggests loss of civic status and exile, and furthermore is abhorred by the "Graces."[9] An ancient commentary on Virgil's Aeneid points out that only Roman matrons wore head bands, for this attire was not permitted to prostitutes.[10]

Polybius (second century BC) reports an act of hostility in which the mother-in-law of Tlepolemus was dragged by his enemies from a temple and paraded through the streets unveiled (*akataluptos*) to prison. The express purpose was to show contempt for her son-in-law and to humiliate him by exposing her head to the public gaze. The citizenry was so infuriated by this outrage that there was a vehement outcry. Although they had endured many other atrocities, this single act galvanized them into public outcry and resistance.[11]

Demonstrably the matter of women's hair and head covering was a matter of deep concern to the entire Christian community and led to concerted action. Thus Paul declares that man and woman belong together in

95

the presence of the Lord, but that there should be suitable propriety lest even the angels[12] (not to mention talebearers[13]) be shocked! Women, both then and now, are affirmed in their desire to exercise the gifts of prophecy: edification, encouragement, and exhortation—but to do so with discretion and respect for the sensibilities of others.

As an introduction to the topic of feminine attire and deportment in general (1 Cor 11:2-16), the apostle turns to the Genesis 1 and 2 account. Man is source (head) of woman as Christ is source of every man, and God is source of Christ.[14] That the word "head" here indicates "source" or "point of origin" is indicated by the twofold statement that woman was drawn out of man (vv. 8, 12). Just as the Son is of the same substance as the Father, woman is of the very same substance as man, a divine gift of blessing, made to be his colleague and confidante (v. 9). At least one of the early church Fathers possessed a text of Genesis 2:18 in which God is recorded to have said, "It is not good for man to be alone. Let us make for him a helper like unto him, an advisor."[15] Her intelligence and spiritual insights are valuable assets.

Woman is indeed a precious gift, to walk beside the man as an equal (1 Cor 11:11-12) and to offer guidance along the way. Paul declares that woman was made "for the sake" of man (v. 9), using the same vocabulary term as he does in saying that Christ "for our sakes" was made poor (2 Cor 8:9). Paul often used this phrase to apply to himself: he made himself an example "for your sakes"(1 Cor 4:6), became a fool "for Christ's sake" (1 Cor 4:10) and a slave "for Jesus' sake"(2 Cor 4:5), and he was given up to death "for Jesus' sake" (2 Cor 4:11). Furthermore, the law is written "for our sake" (1 Cor 9:10), and Paul declared "everything is for your sake" (2 Cor 4:15). The phrase "for the sake of" implies ministry and not inferiority. In no way is it demeaning.

The First Epistle to the Corinthians is addressed to a congregation fraught with conflict and still struggling to free itself from pagan patterns (cf. 1 Cor 12:2). Thus Paul dealt with ritual drunkenness, feasts in pagan temples, sexual promiscuity, eating meat offered to idols, and ritual shouting. Similarly, the letters to Timothy and Titus confront a distressing set of problems besetting the churches in Ephesus and Crete.

The First and Second Epistles to Timothy and Titus use the same vocabulary, address the same themes, and face the same problems. These letters are known as the Pastoral Epistles, with the major emphasis being on advice to church leaders on how to deal with false teaching and wrong conduct within the church. Apparently the same heresy was present in both Ephesus and

Crete, for Paul had left Timothy behind in Ephesus to stop certain individuals from teaching another doctrine (1 Tim 1:3), and Titus was to appoint elders who could stop the false teaching that was wreaking havoc in Crete (Titus 1:9-11).

In point of fact, we know a considerable amount about these difficulties and the opponents who withstood Paul's proclamation of the truth. Astonishingly enough, we even know the names of some of the false teachers (1 Tim 1:20; 2 Tim 2:17-18; 4:14-15). A rundown of the issue of false teachers would include many references: Acts 20:29-30; 1 Corinthians 16:8-9; 1 Timothy 1:3-11, 19-20; 4:1-10; 6:3-5, 20 ff.; 2 Timothy 1:15; 2:14, 16-18, 23; 3:1-9, 13; 4:3-4; Titus 1:10-16; 3:9-11; and Revelation 2:2, 6.

Now it is in the Pastoral Epistles that we find Paul's famous mandate against women teaching (1 Tim 2:12).[16] Does this apply to all women everywhere, or had it to do with a specific situation? Was it intended to prohibit women from teaching wrong doctrine at Ephesus? Let us begin by asking the nature of the false teaching that was being promulgated.

In the first place, it was somehow based on myths. "Instruct them not to be preoccupied with myths" (1 Tim 1:4), Paul wrote to Timothy. He also cautioned, "Avoid profane myths told by old women" (1 Tim 4:7). The stories, whatever they were, led people away from the truth of the Scriptures. "They will turn aside from heeding the truth and stray after myths" (2 Tim 4:4). Strangely enough, these tales had a Hebrew basis, for Paul wrote to Titus, "Rebuke them so that they may be sound in their faith, not preoccupied with Jewish myths and commandments of people who have turned aside from the truth" (Titus 1:14). The stories, then, although dealing with Jewish subjects, ran counter to the truth. We are not talking about Bible stories but about "upside downings" that distorted the truth (Acts 20:30). We do indeed know of such teachers in the early days of Christianity, and we even know something of the stories that they circulated.

These were stories that deliberately subverted the biblical texts and exalted Satan rather than the God of the Scriptures. Thus we read of those whom Paul had "delivered over to Satan so that they may learn not to blaspheme" (1 Tim 1:20). These false teachers were called "knowers" or "Gnostics," and Paul warns not to have anything to do with oppositions of knowledge (*gnosis*) falsely so called (1 Tim 6:20-21). First John also deals with these false "knowers" and how to find the true knowledge that is in Christ.

Gnosticism is sometimes called a religion of rebellion because it deliberately distorts what the Bible teaches, sometimes even declaring "not as Moses said" (cf. 2 Tim 3:8). While many Gnostics turned the Genesis stories upside down in different ways, there was a consistent rejection of the biblical account. Often heaven was peopled with higher powers, some far mightier than the God who created the world in Genesis.[17] According to Gnostic writings, Eve was one of these preexistent powers when Adam was a lifeless lump of clay.[18] Still preserved are several Gnostic accounts of how Eve gives life to Adam:

> Sophia sent Zoe, her daughter, who is called "Eve (of Life)," as an instructor to raise up Adam, in whom there was no soul, so that those whom he would beget might become vessels of light. When Eve saw her co-likeness cast down, she pitied him, and said, "Adam, live! Rise up on the earth!" Immediately her word became a deed. For when Adam rose up, immediately he opened his eyes. When he saw her, he said, "You will be called 'the mother of the living' because you are the one who gave me life."[19]

Here we see a distortion of Eve's role: she preexists Adam, is a celestial power, and breathes the breath of life into Adam.[20] According to Genesis 2:7, it was God who breathed life into the man. Thus Eve becomes a powerful religious force in Gnostic teachings.[21]

Now if we look at Paul's famous prohibition against women teaching (1 Tim 2:12), we note that it is followed by the comment, "Adam was created first, then Eve"(1 Tim 2:13). Does this mean that women are inferior because they were created second, or is this verse a refutation of heretical teaching? The latter seems so.

Next follows a statement about Adam not being deceived and of Eve being absolutely duped (1 Tim 2:14). Some people consider this an explanation as to why women may not teach men, but it may be better understood as a continuation of the refutation of Gnostic beliefs. The Gnostics taught that Adam had been created by a mean and rather stupid deity, who instructed him not to eat of the tree of "knowledge" to prevent him from understanding spiritual truth.

> The first Archon [Ialdeboath] brought Adam [created by the Archons] and placed him in paradise which is said to be a "delight" for him: that is, he intended to deceive him. For their [the Archons'] delight is bitter and their beauty is lawless. Their

delight is deceit and their tree was hostility. Their fruit is poison against which there is no cure, and their promise is death to him. Yet their tree was planted as "tree of life": I shall disclose to you the mystery of their "life"—it is their Counterfeit Spirit, which originated from them so as to turn him away, so that he might not know his perfection.[22]

The Gnostic interpretation of creation included a deliberate deception of Adam by his creator, and enlightenment brought by Eve and the serpent. Eve became an instructor of the highest spiritual "knowledge"[23] that made her and Adam wiser than the Creator.[24] Of course this is a complete reversal of the biblical account. The Bible tells us that God was faithful and true in warning Adam of the consequences of disobedience, and the serpent deceived Eve into making a choice that was terribly wrong (Gen 3:13; 2 Cor 11:3). While heretics glorified Eve and the serpent,[25] Paul warned against the evil of such doctrines.

Such teaching must be stopped. "Prohibit their teaching a different doctrine" (1 Tim 1:3), said Paul. Some of the false teachers had been "delivered to Satan so that they may learn not to blaspheme" (1 Tim 1:20). "They must be silenced, for they disrupt whole households by teaching what they ought not for the sake of shameful gain" (Titus 1:11). "Be severe in correcting them so that they stop giving heed to myths and the commandments of people who have turned aside from the truth" (Titus 1:13).

Along with these commands is placed the directive, "I do not allow a woman to teach or to have authority (*authentein*) over a man; she is to keep silent" (1 Tim 2:12). Can this be a prohibition against heretical teaching on the part of women? Unquestionably women had been swept into the error. Some of the false teachers insinuated themselves into private houses and led forth silly little women, laden with lusts, ever learning and never able to come to a "knowledge" of the truth (2 Tim 3:6-7). We have already spoken of the myths told by "older women," though many translations of the New Testament fail to let the reader know that this is what the text actually says.[26] We read also of younger widows who have "gone astray after Satan" and who "go about from house to house saying what they ought not" (1 Tim 5:15).[27]

Thus it is crucial that we approach this prohibition against women teaching (1 Tim 2:12) with great care. If a woman is not to teach a man, why did Priscilla teach Apollos so that he could reason with great power that Jesus was indeed the Christ (Acts 18:24-28)?[28] Why was Timothy instructed by his mother and grandmother (2 Tim 1:5)? Why are women encouraged to prophesy (1 Cor 11:5)? Why are all Christians to teach and admonish one another (Col 3:16; 1 Cor 14:26)? If we do not believe that Scripture contradicts Scripture, then we must look closely at this prohibition against women teaching.

First of all, Paul insists that women may learn "in silence and submission" (1 Tim 2:11). This is an ancient formula that indicates willingness to listen to what is said and to obey.[29] Unlike many Hebrew women of the day, Christian women are to be taught the word of God so that they may come to a "full knowledge of the truth" (1 Tim 2:4).

The next phrase is more difficult. "To teach I do not permit a woman," writes Paul, "nor to *authentein* a man" (1 Tim 2:12). But what does *authentein* mean, and how are we to translate it? This word occurs only once in the entire New Testament, though it had several different meanings elsewhere in Greek literature, including that of ruling or dominating. Its original meaning was that of killing someone, and surely we do not want a Christian woman to kill a man. It could at times have a sexual nuance, but during the New Testament times it usually meant to begin something or to be responsible for starting something.

The noun form, *authentes*, was used to indicate the following: the author of a speech;[30] the author and introducer of a new legislation;[31] the originator and prime mover of gospel activity;[32] and the author of such laws and words.[33] The word occurs quite frequently in Gnostic and magic texts—one well-known Gnostic of first-century Ephesus worshiped a god whom he called *Authentia*.

The verbal form *authentein* (1 Tim 2:12) also had the meaning of being an author or originator. Some examples include to bring into being;[34] to take the initiative;[35] to originate all things;[36] to be responsible for the deed;[37] to be an instigator of dissension;[38] and to proclaim oneself the author of judgment.[39] Medieval and renaissance scholars concurred about these meanings. William Bude quotes an ancient rhetorician who supplied a definition: "He asserts by such an appellation that this once meant the one who murders with his own hand. Later indeed, and for over a thousand years, *authenteo* in Greek began to signify that which among the speakers of Latin means one who acts or brings about the existence [of anything]."[40]

Nineteenth-century dictionaries listed the meaning "to maintain oneself author of something."[41] When Greek-English dictionaries first appeared, John Pickering noted a meaning when the verb was used with a gentive: "to declare one's self the author or source of anything."[42] And *authentein* is indeed used with a genitive in 1 Timothy 2:12. If we adopt this meaning, we should read 1 Timothy 2:12-13 in this way: "I do not allow a woman to teach or profess herself the author of man, but to be in submission [rather than opposition to the word of God] . . . for Adam was formed first, then Eve, and Adam was not deceived. . . ."

This appears to be far more faithful to Scripture than maintaining that women cannot teach because of Eve's sin or because of women's supposed gullibility. Let us remember that it was a woman prophet who proclaimed the good news of the Messiah's birth to "all who awaited the redemption in Jerusalem"(Luke 2:36-38). It was women whom the Savior sent to proclaim the joyous news of the resurrection (John 20:18).

If we maintain that the text prohibits women in leadership roles over men (see chapter 6), we must explain Deborah who judged Israel, Phoebe who was an overseer in the church at Cenchrae, and Priscilla, a fellow-laborer to whom Paul called others to be subject (Rom 16:3; 1 Cor 16:16).

We must seek an understanding that allows Scripture to be consistent with other Scriptures, especially those that call on all believers to serve Christ to the utmost of their abilities. Women must teach truth, in submission to the word of God, and they must search the Scriptures diligently to make sure that they are not in error.

But what of the perplexing ending to the second chapter of 1 Timothy? Are women really saved through childbearing (2:15)? Many explanations have been attempted, but it is most logical to consider verse 15 an extension of the refutation of Gnostic beliefs. There are ancient texts that call on women to cast off their femininity and become male.[43] In the Gospel of Thomas, the most famous Gnostic document, we read: "Simon Peter said to them: 'Let Mary go out from among us, because women are not worthy of life.' Jesus said, 'Behold, I myself will draw her so that I shall make her into a male in order for her to become as a living spirit like you males, because every woman who will make herself male shall enter into the kingdom of heaven.'"[44]

Certain Gnostic groups decried women bringing children into the world.[45] One sect even forcibly aborted women who became pregnant.[46] According to the Gospel of the Egyptians, Jesus had said that death would end and his kingdom would come when women stopped bearing children.[47]

Paul wrote of heretics who forbade marriage (1 Tim 4:3), but he encouraged young widows both to marry and to have children (1 Tim 5:14). He affirmed women as sexual beings capable of bearing children, while one

Gnostic urged, "flee from the bondage of femininity and choose for your-selves the salvation of masculinity."[48]

But Paul the apostle argues for the full validity of women's salvation within their ability to bear children. Women will be saved "within" their role as child-bearers (*dia*, the word translated "through," can also mean "within") if they continue in faith and love and holiness exercised with propriety. They need not renounce their feminine distinctives. Here then is salvation by a woman's faith and not by her childbearing. Here then is another summons to women for Christ-honoring service.

So, was Paul a friend or foe of females? Many assume the prohibitions Paul uttered about female roles in the church and the home reflect the words of a male chauvinist. At best, they say, Paul simply reflects the social attitudes toward women common to his day.

However, when the texts are investigated and interpreted in light of the cultural context, the writer of thirteen books in the New Testament actually reflects the same revolutionary attitude toward women as did Jesus. Rather than being a subjugator of woman, Paul was a liberator—his words to women, as well as his relationships with them, reveal clearly that he was indeed a supporter and exhorter of women in the New Testament. ✝

NOTES

[1] Plutarch, *Mor.* 909 A.

[2] Ammonius, *Diff.* 1st–2nd century AD. As distinct from *legein*: see Romans 3:19; Plutarch *Alcibiades* XIII, 1-2 (c. 100 AD); Eupolis 95; Demosthenes 21.118. As the opposite of articulate speech, see Theocritus 5.34.

[3] Of the singing voice Eph 5:19; of thunder Rev 10:3-4; as a dragon Rev 13:11; of a trumpet Rev 4:1; of a dead man Heb 11:4; and others.

[4] Aristophanes, *Lysistrata* 627.

[5] For *lalein* as an activity in mystery cults, see Plutarch *Mor.* 81 E; Clement of Alexandria *Prot.* II, 19 (c. 200 AD).

[6] Anne Carson, "Putting Her in Her Place: Woman, Dirt and Desire" in *Before Sexuality: The Construction of Erotic Experience in the Ancient Greek World*, eds. David M. Halperin, John J. Winkler, and Froma I. Zeitlin (Princeton: University Press, 1990), 160.

[7] The word used is *akatakaluptos,* in the Septuagint at Leviticus 13:45 for loosened hair. The Septuagintal rendering of the trial for adultery demands that the woman stand *akataluptos.*

[8] Daniel and Susanna, 31-32, NEB.

[9] Sappho 98b LP; 81b LP.

[10] *Errant solarum matronarum nam meretricibus non davantur.* Servius on Aeneid VII.403.fol. 128 v.

[11] Polybius XV.27.1.

[12] *Angelos* can mean an angel, but the basic meaning is "messenger."

[13] Acts 18:7 reveals the synagogue was adjacent to the meeting place of the church— how easy for gossip to spread!

[14] For an excellent discussion of equality in the Trinity and in gender relations, see Kevin Giles, *The Trinity and Subordination: The Doctrine of God and the Contemporary Gender Debate* (Downers Grove: InterVarsity Press, 2002).

[15] Quodvultdeus, *Book of the Promises and Prophecies of God.* Book 1, p.3.

[16] For a thorough examination of the passage, see Richard Clark Kroeger and Catherine Clark Kroeger, *I Suffer Not A Woman: Rethinking 1 Timothy 2:11-15 In Light of Ancient Evidence* (Grand Rapids: Baker, 1992).

[17] "When they ate, they became acquainted with that power which is superior to all, and they revolted from those who had made them" (Irenaeus 1.30.7).

[18] "Then (the Life)-Eve, since *she existed as a power,* laughed at their intention" (*On the Origin of the World.* II, 5, 116, 26-27, Nag Hammadi Library [NHL], 173). An extensive library of Gnostic materials was discovered at Nag Hammadi in Egypt and is now available in English translation.

[19] NHL, 172.

[20] *Reality of the Archons* (II, 4) 89.11-16.

[21] Hippolytus tells how Eve was venerated in *Refutations* V, 16.9ff.

[22] *Apocryphon of John,* 55:18-56:17, trans. Till (Jonas, 92).

[23] "The Hebrews call his mother 'Eve of life,' i.e. . . . . 'the instructor of life'" (*The Origin of the World* 113:33-114:3 [NHL, 171]).

[24] Epiphanius speaks of a heretical Gospel of Eve. It was, he says, named after her because she "discovered the food of *gnosis* [divine acquaintance] through revelation spoken to her by the snake (Epiphanius, *Panarion* 26.2.6).

[25] "They give honor to Eve as the first to eat of the tree of knowledge (*gnosis)* and ordain bishops, elders, and priests because of Eve" (Epiphanius, *Panarion* XLIX).

[26] The Greek term *graodes* means "pertaining or belonging to an aged woman."

[27] Cf. with the false teacher of Thyatira (Rev 2:24).

[28] Note Paul's commendation of Priscilla in 2 Tim 4:19.

[29] James Pritchard, *Ancient Near Eastern Texts Relating to the Old Testament* (Princeton: University Press, 1950), 379, 381.

[30] Gregory of Nyssa, *Antirrheticus adversus Apolinarium,* ed. Mueller, *Gregorii Nysseni opera, vol. 3.1.166.30.*

[31] Eusebius, *The Proof of the Gospel* 1.7.1.4.

[32] Ibid., 3.1.3.5.

[33] Ibid., 3.6.29.

[34] Athanasius, *Testimonia e scriptura (de communie essentia patris et filii et spiritus sancti)* (Migne 28.41.41).

[35] Basil, *Epistle* 69.1.37.

[36] Epiphanius, Haer, 37.2.

[37] John Chrysostom, *Homily on Acts III.3* (Migne 9.26 D).

[38] Leo the Great, *Epistle 30* (Migne PL 54.788A).

[39] Eusebius, *Life of Constantine* 2.48 (Migne 20.1025C).

[40] Guillaume Bude citing Theodore of Gaza's *De Mensibus* in *Commentarii linguae Graecae* (Paris: 1831–1865).

[41] H. Stephanus, *Thesaurus Graecae Linguae,* 8 vols., ed. Dindorf (Paris: 1831–1865), s.v.

[42] John Pickering, *A Greek and English Lexicon adapted to the Authors Read in the Colleges and Schools of the Unitied States and to Other Greek Classics,* 2d ed. (Boston: 1829), s.v.

[43] First Apocalypse of James, *Nag Hammadi Codex 5.3.41.15-16.* The Gospel of Mary, *Codex Berlinensis Gnosticus* 1.9.15-50.

[44] *Gospel of Thomas,* Logion 114.

[45] Stephen Benko, "The Libertine Gnostic Sect of the Phibionites According to Epiphanius," *Vigiliae Christianae* 21, 2 (1967) 103-19.

[46] Epiphanius, *Panarion* 26.5 (Migne PG 41.340).

[47] Clement of Alexandria, *Miscellanies* 3.45, 63-64 (Migne PG 8.1.1193).

[48] Zostrianos, 8.1.131, 5-8.

CHAPTER NINE

God and Gender:

Is God Male or Female? Both or Neither?

Sheri Adams

I checked out books from the local library recently to read to my three-year-old grandson. One of the books had God as a character in the story. God was an old man with a long white beard, dressed in khaki pants and a plaid shirt. When my own daughter was about that age, she had a Bible called *The Beginner's Bible*. There was a picture for each Bible story. For the Genesis 1 account of creation ("So God created humankind in his image, in the image of God he created them; male and female he created them," v. 27), there was a picture of a man. For the Genesis 2 account, there was a picture of a man and a woman. The caption read: "God is male. God created the man first. God created the woman to be the man's helper." This powerful conditioning starts early and is very pervasive. For many people it determines the way they read the Bible, think about God, and relate to one another as men and women for the rest of their lives.

At this point it is tempting to say that it is obvious to all that God is not literally male. Jesus told the Samaritan woman, "God is spirit" (John 4:24), perhaps meaning that God is not literally on your mountain or ours. Since Jesus is not talking about God as a ghost, "God is spirit" would seem to rule out maleness, or femaleness, in our thinking about God.

The reality is quite different. I have asked many, many people what image they had of God when they were children. Almost to a person, people have responded that they thought of God in male terms, either like their fathers or simply as a man. Most of the people reading this chapter have sat through countless worship services in which every reference to God in the service was in male terms: he, him, his, Father, King, Lord.

Every statement we make about God, every picture we produce of God, is an interpretation of God. This is a crucial point to recognize because from our interpretations come our theology and from our theology comes our guidelines for the Christian life. This is nowhere more evident at the moment than in the controversy that has divided Southern Baptists for twenty-plus years. One group stresses Genesis 1, the words and actions of Jesus, and Paul's ideal vision for the church, arguing for equality and mutuality between men and women in all areas of life. Another group emphasizes Genesis 2, 3, and 4, Paul's commands to females, and the domestic codes of the New Testament, arguing for the leadership of the man in the home and church. Each side has interpreted not only Jesus, Paul, and the Bible, but God as well. We have defined God differently, and therefore have developed different guidelines for the living of our lives.

Theology and ethics are inseparable. One informs and reinforces the other. We see this clearly in Southern Baptist life. Jim Richards is the executive director of the newly-formed Southern Baptists of Texas Convention. It was reported that Dr. Richards, in his inaugural address to that group in 1998, said, "God is eternal, all-powerful, all-knowing, holy and male. He is a gender-specific being."[1]

In email conversation with this writer, Dr. Richards said, "I reviewed the tapes of the sermon from the inaugural message. I did not say 'male.' I did say, 'God is eternal, all-powerful, all knowing and holy. He is a gender-specific being.' I have made the following statement, 'God is sexless in His essence, but has chosen to reveal Himself through maleness to humankind.'"

To the question, "How can God, who is sexless in essence, be gender-specific, except in Jesus?" Dr. Richards responded, "Although the scripture uses various similes, metaphors and other figures of speech to describe God, God has chosen to use male expressions in revelatory nomenclature. Jesus called God, 'Father.' Masculine pronouns are used for God. Scriptures present a Father-child relationship between God and his children. Nowhere does the Scripture indicate that God should be referred to as 'our Mother.' It is my understanding that God is gender-specific in Jesus Christ and in the choice of self-descriptive revelatory language."[2] In this chapter, I seek to respond to the interpretation of God reflected in these statements.

As we have said, theology affects ethics. The website of the Council on Biblical Manhood and Womanhood serves as an apologetic tool to promote a traditionalist understanding of female subordination. Recently the site posted a "Statement of Concern about the TNIV Bible." One sentence in the statement read, "We wonder how the TNIV translators can be sure that this masculine language in God's very words does not carry meaning that God wants us to see."[3]

I asked for further elaboration and received the following reply: "[I]t is perhaps no accident but entirely appropriate for the Bible to use representative masculine language. Given the fact that Scripture presents the representative character of Adam as head of the human race, *of men as heads of their families* [my italics], and of Christ as head of his people, this representative masculine language to express a general truth that applies to both men and women is appropriate and perhaps should be expected."[4]

Actions of the Southern Baptist Convention (SBC) over the last twenty years (particularly the 1984 statement on women, the 2000 *Baptist Faith and Message* statements on women, and the isolation of woman into special programs at seminaries) indicate that this is the view of the present leadership of the SBC. The question of female equality is determining the policy of seminaries and boards, and people who do not agree are being fired or forced out.

Gail Ramshaw deals with the need for theological interpretation in her splendid book, *God beyond Gender*.[5] We are trying with our words to convey something about God. Words are the only tools we have to do this, but words are also the problem. Some words do a good job of describing God; some don't. With the passage of time and the changes in language, words that may have worked well at one time no longer do so. It is both important and sobering to realize that some words, even though they are biblical words, may lead us away from the truth we are trying to convey.

Ramshaw is right. I am reminded of a remark made by Gerald Keown, who teaches Old Testament and is my colleague at Gardner-Webb. "There are more references to God as Warrior in the Old Testament than any other reference," he said, "and I'm concerned about people who aren't concerned about that!" The Old Testament is filled with references to God as Warrior, yet Jesus told his disciples to be peacemakers (Matt 5:9) and said, "All who take the sword will also perish by the sword" (Matt 26:52). So the language of God as Warrior does not by itself help us understand the full nature of God as revealed in Jesus.[6]

BIBLICAL IMAGES FOR GOD

In an Introduction to Theology class, the students and I searched the Bible for one thing: the use of figurative language to describe God. What we found was important. There are at least sixty-seven different word pictures, or word portraits, used by the biblical writers of the Old Testament to describe God.

For example, God is compared to animals: a lion, a leopard, a wild animal, or a bear robbed of her cubs. Phrases from nature are used to describe God: the dew to Israel, an evergreen cypress, a cloud, or the sun. Word portraits that convey strength are popular: God is a rock, the rock of my salvation, the rock of my refuge, a strong tower, a shield, or a stronghold. Occupations are often used to describe God. God is portrayed as a landowner, a potter, a judge, a shepherd, and a sower of grain.

Words that denote family relationships are also used: God is described as helper and like a husband, father, and mother. God is our creator, defender, deliverer, protector, redeemer, refuge, and savior. God is one, the mighty one. God is the God of Israel, the God of hosts, God of the whole earth, and the God of Gods.

The class members and I also found sixty-plus word portraits for God and/or Jesus in the New Testament. Again, images from the natural and animal world are utilized: Lamb, Lamb of God, Light of the world, Lion of Judah, and Vine. Many word portraits are used to emphasize Jesus' unique life and ministry: Alpha and Omega, First Born of the Dead, King of Kings, Lord of Lords, and Son of the Most High God.

The writers of the Bible piled up word pictures in an attempt to portray with words what cannot be portrayed with mere words. God is beyond our ability to describe. All word portraits used to describe God are figurative. *All language to describe God is figurative language.* It is not difficult to think of some of the word portraits as figurative. God is obviously not really a mother bear robbed of her cubs or a green pine tree. It is more difficult to think of other word portraits as figurative for three reasons: (1) our familiarity with the images conveyed by the word portraits; (2) the conditioning toward certain language for God most of us have received in our churches; and (3) God is more like (in our theology anyway) certain images or word portraits than others.

For instance, God, we believe, is more like a human being than a rock or a leopard. So God is more like a human parent than God is like a bear robbed of her cubs. When we say, however, that God is like a human father or like a human mother, we do not intend to say that God is a male or a female. Rather we say the Bible portrays God as being like a human father and like a human mother in order to speak of God's character and concern.

FEMININE IMAGES FOR GOD

I wish to define as carefully as I can the understanding I have of "female" and of "feminine." By "female," I am talking about biology. For our purposes, we will define females as humans who are biologically so. With "feminine," we are dealing with culture. Culture tells us what is "masculine" and what is "feminine." Writers of dictionary definitions have tended to reflect the culture, which reinforces stereotypes.

There are few activities that are exclusively "female." Having children and nursing them are obvious ones. Likewise, there are few activities that are exclusively "male." Women obviously cannot impregnate anyone. In reality, however, beyond an extremely small number of activities, men and women can basically do the same things. Some men and women can do some things better, faster, and longer than other men and women, but basically most of us can do more or less the same things. Culture dictates, in large measure, what women and men can, should, or must do or not do.

Lately, many Baptists have idealized an earlier time when things seemed better. In that "better time," women's roles and a woman's place were more clearly defined and accepted. We create problems, however, when we read into the Bible and the biblical cultures this imaginary culture we have idealized. Our cultural ideals can actually blind us to what is actually in the Bible, and we assume a setting that was not there.

It would be foolish to claim that there is an abundance of material in the Bible that portrays God as female or in feminine metaphors. There isn't. Given the fact, however, that the world of the Bible was a patriarchal society (often with a vengeance), the amazing thing is that such analogies exist at all. In fact, it would almost lead one to believe that the only reason feminine pictures of God do exist is because the Bible is divinely inspired.

In Luke 15, God is portrayed as a father who longs for his prodigal son's return, as a shepherd (who sometimes were females, like Rachel) searching for a lost sheep, and as a woman who had lost a precious coin.[7] Jesus once described himself as feeling like a mother hen concerned for her brood, when Christ he over Jerusalem's spiritual rebellion (Matt 23:37; Luke 13:34).

The prophet Isaiah beautifully described God's motherly love and comfort: "Sing for joy, O heavens, and exult, O earth; break forth, O mountains, into singing! For the LORD has comforted his people, and will have compassion on his suffering ones. But Zion said, 'The LORD has forsaken me, my LORD has forgotten me.' Can a woman forget her nursing child, or show no compassion for the child of her womb? Even these may forget, yet I will not forget you" (Isa 49:13-15).

In the last chapter of his prophetic book, Isaiah once again likens God to a mother who comforts her child Israel by restoring Jerusalem. The nation will be able to nurse to its heart's content; and God's children will be carried around and bounced on "Mama" Jerusalem's knees (66:11-12). Israel will be loved, nursed, and cared for by Jerusalem's God, for "As a mother comforts her child, so I will comfort you; you shall be comforted in Jerusalem" (66:13).

The psalmist portrays a deeply personal, feminine picture of God in the role of a midwife: "Yet it was you who took me from the womb; you kept me safe on my mother's breast. On you I was cast from my birth, and since my mother bore me you have been my God" (22:9-11). Here God serves as a midwife, or possibly a nurse or a nanny.[8] God delivers the infant and presents the baby to its mother, but notice it is God on whom the child has relied.

Surely, however, the most graphic and compelling portrayals of God as likened to a female in the Bible are those in which God is portrayed as giving birth.[9] In an interesting passage, God is portrayed first as a soldier-warrior; then God is immediately pictured as a woman in labor, gasping and panting. "The LORD goes forth like a soldier, like a warrior he stirs up his fury; he cries out, he shouts aloud, he shows himself mighty against his foes. For a long time I have held my peace, I have kept still and restrained myself; now I will cry out like a woman in labor, I will gasp and pant" (Isa 42:13-14).

Deuteronomy 32 recounts the story of Israel's unfaithfulness to God. "You were unmindful of the Rock that bore you; you forgot the God who gave you birth" (32:18). Phyllis Trible interprets this verse as "the God who writhed in labor pains with you."[10] God is depicted here as like a mother who is laboring to give birth to a child.

One of the most fascinating analogies of God is found in Numbers 11:10-13. "Moses heard the people weeping throughout their families, all at the entrances of their tents. Then the LORD became very angry, and Moses was displeased. So Moses said to the LORD, 'Why have you treated your servant so badly? Why have I not found favor in your sight, that you lay the burden of all this people on me? Did I conceive all this people? Did I give birth to them, that you should say to me, 'Carry them in your bosom, as a nurse carries a sucking child,' to the land that you promised on oath to their ancestors?'"

Moses was discouraged. These rebellious people were not his responsibility; they were God's problem. Jehovah was the One who had conceived and birthed them, and like a mother nursing a child, God should care for Israel.[11]

110

To summarize, "In various passages, God conceives, is pregnant, writhes in labor pains, brings forth a child, and nurses it . . . such language expands, broadens, and deepens our understanding of the biblical God."[12] These images of God as like a female may sound strange and radical because most of us are not used to hearing God depicted in this way. It is important to remember that the analogy does not mean that God was really pregnant, really gave birth, or really nursed.

In the same way, when we call God "Father", we are not saying that God really impregnated a woman who bore God a son. In fact, it was that false religious idea that the biblical writers condemned. Fertility cults were common in the nations surrounding Israel.

Nevertheless, the analogy of father and the analogy of mother, rightly understood, are the best analogies we have for God. No analogy can say everything. The comparison of human relationships of any kind with God is limited by human sin. But even so, God is more like a caring human father or a loving mother than God is like anything else we can describe. So, even with these limitations, we can still retain the analogy of God as mother and father.

JESUS' PORTRAYAL OF GOD

Jesus' mission was "to reveal the very character and purpose of God."[13] The life of Jesus brought the nature of God into focus. Jesus said in John 17:26, "I have made your name known . . . so that the love with which you have loved me may be in them, and I in them." However, Jesus' life, words, and actions must be interpreted. Everything we find in the Bible that happened before Jesus and everything that happened after Jesus should be filtered through the life of Jesus that we find in the four Gospels.

Even after we admit that, because we are so familiar (we think) with the life of Jesus, we often miss seeing just how much Jesus challenged the status quo. By the standards of his day, Jesus was a liberal Jew.[14] This was especially true in his treatment of women. Remember, Jesus' actions inform us of God's character and purpose.

In the first-century world, "Women were profoundly second-class citizens."[15] It is not out of line to compare the similarities between the women of that culture and Afghan women under the Taliban. The lines of separation were clearly drawn in both. In neither culture could a woman receive an education. In both, they had to be covered from head to toe in public. Females were locked out of the religious hierarchy in both societies. And in both, men basically made all the decisions and ruled over the women and children. This was and is patriarchy.

Marcus Borg wrote, "All of the stories about Jesus and women in the Gospels constitute a radical challenge to patriarchy."[16] Many times Jesus astonished his disciples by doing what to us seems ordinary. He struck up conversations with women or allowed them to talk to him. Some of the Pharisees of Jesus' day would not speak to female members of their own families in public.

Jesus allowed women to touch him, even women considered "untouchable," like the woman with the hemorrhaging of blood. And to the amazement of onlookers, he touched them. He sometimes did the unthinkable, such as when he touched a dead person out of his compassion for the widow of Nain (Luke 7:11-17). At another time Jesus commended Mary for acting unladylike by sitting at his feet and learning (Luke 10:42). Jesus included women among his disciples and accepted money from them for his ministry (Luke 8:1-3). Quite simply, Jesus loved his women friends and they loved him.[17]

It is especially important to interpret the life of the early church in the New Testament by the life and teachings of the founder of that church, Jesus. In many ways the earliest Christians struggled to understand Jesus, even at times failing to live up to the model laid out for them. Jesus included, while the church gradually excluded. In fact, the early church ended up dismissing much of Jesus' teaching as "impractical." Perhaps "dismissing" is too strong a word, but they certainly reinterpreted much of Jesus' teaching to fit the cultural standards and expectations of their day. This is first detected in the New Testament church described in the Bible. In the emerging church in the book of Acts, female roles were not a major issue. Women were disciples—no more, no less. In fact, the doors were so wide open at first that it took a great deal of time and theological maneuvering to get them closed. We see this beginning to happen in the New Testament. As cultural traditions and Christian ideals clashed, the early church knuckled under on the issue of equality for slaves and women. Yet, even as the New Testament era closed, women were still in positions of leadership, as they continued to be for quite some time.

In today's ongoing debate about the place and role of women in ministry, some have argued that ministry should be limited to men because God became incarnate in the male person, Jesus of Nazareth. That Jesus was a male is without dispute. Yet, it doesn't seem unreasonable to suggest that incarnation was a case in which God had to work within the culture. The incarnation was an accommodation of God to human limitations, weaknesses, and frailties. In this social sense, God had to accommodate to the Jewish and Graeco-Roman culture at that time in history. Given the reality of the social limitations placed upon women, incarnation as a woman was not an option. Who would have heard or followed a woman Messiah?

The important thing to remember is that the incarnation was a one-time event. The issue that we today face is what we learn from the life of Jesus about God and God's plan and purpose for women. The record is clear—Jesus included women, Jesus taught women, Jesus called women, and Jesus sent women forth as proclaimers of the good news.

JESUS AND THE TWELVE

Some make the case that women cannot be senior pastors, or even church ministers, because this role would require them to preach in church, teach mixed groups, stand behind the pulpit, serve as a church minister, exercise authority over males, and so on *ad infinitum*. Why? Because the disciples Jesus called (the Twelve) were all men. One writer laments, "[I]f Jesus had appointed female apostles, then it would be clear that all ministry roles are open to women . . . Jesus seems to accommodate to the culture more than Paul—when he could have made a bold statement that would have resolved the whole issue definitively."[18]

Other Bible scholars counter by arguing that if you follow such reasoning, only non-slave Jewish males are eligible to be pastors of Christian churches today, since that is who Jesus called. Both the argument and the counter argument miss a very important point behind why Jesus elected the Twelve in the first place. Jesus intended the Twelve Apostles to be a symbol. Just as there were twelve patriarchs in the old kingdom of Israel as established by God, now there would be twelve patriarchs in the new Israel, the kingdom established by Jesus. With the symbol of the patriarchs, Jesus demonstrated his intention to form a new nation, a new people—to begin again God's reign, now in the hearts of believers. With the symbol of the twelve disciples, Jesus was saying to the tribes of Israel, "I am the promise of God made to your fathers."[19]

Many of our present questions would be answered if we would simply take Jesus more seriously. What we need to do is to hear Jesus in the context of the world in which he lived. The conservative Jews of Jesus' day were saying to the women, "These things you cannot do," but Jesus was saying, "Yes, you can!"

PORTRAIT OF GOD

We have spoken of the powerful conditioning we receive, beginning at birth, that encourages us to think of God as male or masculine. We have insisted that all descriptions of God are interpretations of God, and indeed the implications of these interpretations are far-reaching in their influence. Also, we have noticed that the Bible uses many images, or word portraits, to describe God, including a number of female or feminine images. In a few passages, God is portrayed as a woman. It is difficult for many people in their thoughts about God to accept these feminine analogies—but they are in the Bible and cannot be dismissed. To ignore these pictures of God is to skew our theology and to corrupt our ethics.

God is neither male nor female. God is God. God has chosen, however, to use images of males and females to picture God's character and nature. God also chose to be depicted as animals and as inanimate objects, like a rock or a tree. No one is tempted to interpret those portraits of God literally. Likewise, we do not interpret male and female portrayals of God literally, but we are informed by these images. In a deeper sense, it is the sum of who we are as male and female that best helps us to understand God.

God, who is neither male nor female, created sexual distinctions for us to relate and to enjoy. My guess is that God is disappointed that we have abused this good gift with our attempts to gain power. Jesus modeled for us God's concern that all barriers—racial, national, and sexual—between men and women be eliminated (Gal 3:28).

Jesus, God in the flesh, was not concerned that women fulfill a role dictated by society, but that each woman find God's will for her life and do it. Luke 11:27-28 records a woman in the crowd crying out to Jesus, "Blessed is the womb that bore you and the breasts that nursed you!" This was the assumed, expected, sanctioned, and approved role for women in that day. Jesus heard her and responded, "Blessed rather are those who hear the word of God and obey it!" To "hear the word of God and obey it" is the first priority of us all—men and women, fathers and mothers, husbands and wives. Each person must hear and obey for themselves; no one can do this for you.

Our interpretation of God's word will not determine how God works in our lives, although our skewed interpretations do make it harder to hear clearly God's voice. God has the authority and freedom to call any person into any ministry.

Our understanding of God would not be complete without a brief discussion of the meaning of Genesis 1:27: "So God created humankind in his image, in the image of God he created them; male and female he created them." We might be wiser to heed Ramshaw's reminder that the Jewish people have not speculated heavily on this "enigmatic phrase from Genesis."[20] The history of the interpretation of the phrase "image of God" illustrates that theologians have tended to define the image of God "from either their conception of God or their hope of humanity."[21] Moreover, we should certainly remember a basic hermeneutical truth: "You can more or less count on it that where there are four to fourteen viable options as to what a text meant, even the scholars are guessing!"[22]

Nevertheless, this text is pivotal and must be addressed. In the opening pages of the Bible, we read that in one act of creation, man and woman are brought into existence. Here it is clear that together they form the image of God. In fact, we have no image of God apart from maleness and femaleness. Together they represent the image of God.[23] Set in its historical context this statement is amazing. In Egypt it was believed that only the Pharaoh was made in the image of God.[24] In the ancient cultures, it was striking that a group of people would assert that every common person was made in the image of God, and indeed absolutely radical to believe that women, as well as men, held that image.

The interpretive challenge is to decide exactly how to understand the Hebrew words "image of God." Is this a picture, a model, a form, or even a shadow or dream? What does this phase mean when translated into our own understanding? Does the author intend to describe some physical likeness to God, or does the idea refer to an inner quality—the will, reason, or moral capacity?[25]

Most scholars agree that the passage speaks of the "dignity" of human beings when compared with animals. It is also clear from the text that this dignity comes from being "God's representative" or being made in the image of God.[26] For our purpose, it is important to note that however defined, both men and women bear this dignity, as well as all the rights, privileges, and responsibilities that go with having been made in the "image of God."

In the New Testament, to speak of the image of God is to speak of Christ. God's will for men and women is to become like Christ, and in that way we will become like God. In Christ, we no longer see a shadow of God, but we see God clearly.

Understanding that male and female comprise the image of God helps us understand why a theology that is too male-centered fails to portray the whole truth of the Bible. A theology that is too "masculine" is not able to speak to the truth that the female bears the image of God with the male. At its worse, it becomes a tool to deny the woman the rights and privileges she has because she is made in the image of God. The corrective is an acknowledgment that the Bible, even though composed in a society that was almost totally andro-centric and patriarchal, manages to reflect a larger truth—"in the image of God he created them; male and female he created them" (Gen 1:27).

I conclude where I began: *All language for God is figurative language.* It has to be. God cannot be fully described in human language. Many of us believe the masculine language for God we find in the Bible reflects the patriarchal culture in which it was written and therefore is not binding. Others believe God used masculine language to teach that the male alone is ordained to be the leader and authority in home and church. Although both groups need to admit that we are both interpreting the Bible, we must also agree that when we interpret the Bible, we must be willing to go as far as the Bible goes: the biblical God is portrayed with male and female imagery.

In addition, those traditionalists who enforce the theology that the man is the head of the house need to be honest enough to admit that this teach-ing is being misunderstood, misapplied, and misused. Some men are convinced that they are superior to women, and some women are equally sure that they are inferior to men. Too many women are being taught that God simply does not relate to them in the same way as God relates to men.

The language that "the man is the head of the home and the church" *assumes* all men will show love, care, and consideration for women under their authority, just as Jesus loved and cared for the church. Jesus taught us to judge a tree by its fruit (Matt 7:20). Look at churches and church leaders who believe in this doctrine of male leadership. Look into the homes of men who follow the belief in male authority. What happens all too often? The love, care, and respect are missing.

Is it biblical to teach females that raising children is the end-all and be-all of a woman's life? Many women, no matter how strong their desire for marriage and family, will not marry. Others are unable to bear children. Should they be made to feel like failures in God's plan for females?

In fact, mothering the young, no matter how many children a woman has, will and must end, especially if we want our children to have lives of their own. Mothering is a very important role, but it is not the only role a woman should play. I am a mother and a teacher. I am a better teacher because I am a mother, and I am a better mother because I teach.

We need to be honest about the powerful role masculine language for God plays in forming people's ideas about God. For those of us who would like to see our children's children develop better understandings of God, we must get serious about changing the way we talk about God. Actually, it is not that hard. Three simple changes will take care of most of our problems. The first is to use "God-is-like" language, especially with children. God is like a father; God is like a mother; God is like . . . . You fill in the blank with the dozens of examples from the Bible. The second change is to cease to use the masculine pronouns "he, him, or his" for God. Just God will do. The only awkward-sounding construction is God's-self for himself, but in time, that awkwardness will disappear. The third change is to warn Christians about women's conferences that promote the idea that God ordained female submission and that women are meant to be under the authority of men.[27]

We must stop misrepresenting Jesus.[28] We must begin to take Jesus seriously. We must take the way Jesus treated women seriously. We must take the example of the early church in Acts seriously. We must take the work and research of biblical scholars seriously.

No man, not even a husband, can accept or reject Jesus Christ for a woman. No man, not even a husband, can die in the place of a woman. No man, not even a husband, can face the Final Judgment for a woman. Because a man cannot do these things for a woman, she must be allowed to relate to God on her own. Every woman can hear the voice of God, can answer the call of God, and can do the will of God.

God is neither male nor female—God is God! For that reason, "There is no longer Jew or Greek, there is no longer slave or free, there is no longer male or female; for all of you are one in Christ Jesus" (Gal 3:28). ✝

NOTES

[1] *Baptist Standard,* 18 November 1998, 9.

[2] Email conversations, 9-22 July 2002.

[3] Council on Biblical Manhood and Womanhood website, 5 June 2002.

[4] Email from Chris Cowan, Academic/Pastoral Web Correspondent, Council on Biblical Manhood and Womanhood, 5 June 2002.

[5] Gail Ramshaw, *God beyond Gender: Feminist Christian God-Language* (Minneapolis: Fortress Press, 1995). I recommend reading this book as well as viewing the bibliography for other resources on this subject.

[6] See Ramshaw, *God beyond Gender,* 101, for other interpretations of God as Warrior.

[7] Letha D. Scanzoni and Nancy A. Hardesty, *All We're Meant to Be* (Nashville: Word, 1974), 29. Dr. Todd D. Still, New Testament professor at Gardner-Webb, noted, "All three parables are about God's concern for people: God is like the father, God is like the shepherd, and God is like the woman."

[8] Ann Loades, ed., *Feminist Theology: A Reader* (Louisville: Westminster, John Knox Press, 1990), 25.

[9] Ann M. Clifford, *Introducing Feminist Theology* (Maryknoll NY: Orbis, 2001), 104; Phyllis Trible, *God and the Rhetoric of Sexuality* (Philadelphia: Fortress Press, 1978), 64.

[10] Trible, 69.

[11] Ibid.

[12] Ibid.

[13] George Buttrick, ed., *Interpreter's Dictionary of the Bible,* vol. 2 (Nashville: Abingdon Press, 1990), 408.

[14] Charles R. Page II, *Jesus and the Land* (Nashville: Abingdon Press, 1995), 62-63.

[15] Hershel Shanks, ed., *The Search for Jesus: Modern Scholarship Looks at the Gospels* (Washington, DC: Biblical Archaeology Society, 1994), 52.

[16] Ibid., 53.

[17] Sherri Adams, *What the Bible Really Says about Women* (Macon GA: Smyth & Helwys, 1994), 72-77.

[18] James R. Beck and Craig L. Blomberg, eds., *Two Views on Women in Ministry* (Grand Rapids: Zondervan, 2001), 196.

[19] Adams, *What the Bible Really Says,* 79-80.

[20] Ramshaw, *God beyond Gender,* 19.

[21] Ibid., 17.

[22] Gordon D. Fee and Douglas Stuart, *How To Read the Bible For All Its Worth* (Grand Rapids: Zondervan, 1982), 60.

[23] Conversation with Dr. Gerald Keown, Professor of Old Testament at Gardner-Webb, 24 July 2002.

[24] Buttrick, *Interpreter's Dictionary,* 683.

[25] Ibid.

[26] Ibid.

[27] See Joe E. Trull, *Walking in the Way: An Introduction to Christian Ethics* (Nashville: Broadman & Holman, 1993), 183, for an illustration of a popular seminar for women that teaches "The Joy of Submission."

[28] See Dorothy Kelley Patterson, *Should Women Serve as Pastors? Should Women Teach or Rule Over Men in the Church?* (Wake Forest NC: Southeastern Baptist Theological Seminary, n.d.).

CHAPTER TEN

Is the Head of the
House at Home?

Joe E. Trull

T he phone rings just as I sit down to dinner. The voice asks, "Is this
the head of the house?" Should my answer be brave or honest? I
reply, "It depends on what you mean by 'head.'"

The answer to the title question is similar. Yes, there is a head of the
house at home, but probably not the one you had in mind. For the Christian
household, Christ is the true head.

Should a wife "submit graciously to the servant leadership of her husband"?[1] According to the Southern Baptist Convention's recent revision of the
Baptist Faith and Message confessional statement, she should. But not according to 69 percent of the respondents to a 1998 Gallup Poll.[2] And not
according to the evangelical community, for the issue of male headship and
female submission in marriage continues to be hotly debated.[3] Two models of
marriage that claim biblical warrant and vie for evangelicals' allegiance focus
on Paul's words to Ephesian believers concerning family responsibilities.

Ephesians 5:21–6:9 is a *Hausentafel* (a code of household duties) and a
central Pauline passage on the Christian home.[4] Often quoted in wedding
ceremonies, these well-worn verses are sometimes used to support a traditional view of male superiority and female submission in marriage
relationships.[5] The thesis of this article is that Ephesians 5:21–6:9 upholds a
model of mutual submission under the lordship of Christ.

Jewish and Gentile moralists commonly wrote guidelines to govern the
behavior of family members. Biblical scholars presume Ephesians 5:21–6:9
was part of catechetical instruction given to new converts in Christian
churches along with other teachings (Col 3:18–4:1; Titus 2:1-10;

1 Pet 2:13–3:7).[6] The Apostle Paul added a new element in his household codes—the Christian home was to be different from the typical Graeco-Roman family. Every member of the Christian family was to live under the lordship of Christ, which revolutionized domestic relationships.

Paul's teachings about the home may have arisen because of the breakdown of the family in the New Testament world. In Jewish families, the wife had no rights at all and was regarded more as a possession than a person. The woman's position in the Greek world was worse, for the wife lived a secluded life. As Xenophon put it, females were to "see as little as possible, hear as little as possible, and ask as little as possible."[7] The Greek way of life made companionship in marriage impossible.

In Rome the matter was even worse. For the first five hundred years the Roman Republic recorded not one case of divorce. By the time of Paul, Roman family life was crumbling. Seneca wrote that women were married to be divorced and divorced to be married. Jerome tells of a woman in Rome who was married to her twenty-third husband and she was his twenty-first wife.[8]

In this atmosphere where adultery was common and chastity rare, Paul was concerned about family breakdown in the churches. In Corinth, for example, some members seemed to overlook an incestuous relationship (1 Cor 5:1-2), while others desired to disavow their marital ties altogether (1 Cor 7).

A few years after Paul wrote to the Corinthians, he counseled Ephesian Christians about marriage and family relationships. Although not himself a married man (1 Cor 7:7), Paul grew up in a devoutly religious childhood home (Phil 3:4-6; 2 Cor 11:22). In addition, Paul had the teachings of Jesus and Jesus' treatment of women and children as background. Out of these circumstances the missionary teacher penned one of the noblest statements in Scripture about marriage and family.

A FOREIGN WORLD[9]

To interpret Paul's domestic teachings correctly, it is absolutely essential to understand family roles and relationships in the first-century world. Although Jewish women occupied a position of dignity and responsibility in the home, in social and religious life they were little more than an appendage of their husbands. A Jewish woman was entirely at the disposal of her father or her spouse. Forbidden to learn the law, she had no part in the synagogue service, she could not teach in school, and she could not testify in the courts. Talking to women in public was forbidden, even between a man and his wife or daughter.

The respectable Greek woman lived a secluded life; confined to her quarters, she did not emerge even for meals. Normally she appeared in public only once or twice per year during religious festivals or at a relative's funeral. The reason for her seclusion is related to the role of the Greek wife. Demosthenes explained the accepted rule: "We have courtesans (*hetairai*) for our pleasure, prostitutes (i.e., young female slaves) for daily physical use, wives to bring up legitimate children and to be faithful stewards in household matters."[10] The wife's primary function was to bear a male heir for her husband; love and companionship were to be found elsewhere.

In Roman society a woman had greater practical freedom. A Roman wife could appear in public with her husband and was allowed by law to initiate divorce, but beyond that her rights were limited. In the Roman pantheon and the Roman theatre, women were thoroughly degraded.[11]

In stark contrast to the universal denigration of females and the deterioration of marriage in the first century, Jesus' attitude was totally counterculture. Sweeping aside centuries of tradition and prejudice, Jesus' treatment of women was revolutionary. What did he do? Christ simply related to women as he did to men, never regarding them as inferior in any way. Christ also reaffirmed God's original intent for marriage, which Paul quotes in this passage: "For this reason a man will leave his father and mother and be joined to his wife, and the two will become one flesh" (Eph 5:31; Matt 19:5).

The Christian faith did much for women, and even more for children. In the Roman world, life was perilous for the child. Under the Roman *patria potestas*, a Roman father had absolute power over his family. Any member could be sold as a slave, be required to work in chains, or even be given the death penalty. The power of the Roman father extended over the whole life of the child, as long as the father lived. Though public opinion seldom allowed it, history records some instances of a Roman father condemning his son and executing him.[12]

Child exposure was also common. When a child was born, the infant was placed at the father's feet. If the father picked up the child, that meant he would keep it. If he walked away, the child was rejected. A Roman child always risked being repudiated and exposed. Unwanted children were often left in the Roman forum, where they were collected and raised by people to be slaves or prostitutes. The sickly or deformed child was treated with even greater cruelty—often drowned, according to Seneca.[13]

Symptomatic of the pervasive moral corruption of the first-century world were not only the common practices of infanticide and the denigration of women, but also slavery. One authority estimated that in the Roman Empire of Paul's day there were 60,000,000 slaves, with 20,000,000 in Italy alone and 650,000 in Rome.[14] Almost all work was done by slaves, for it was beneath the dignity of a Roman citizen to work. The slave was not a person, but a thing. Aristotle taught that slave and master could never be friends, for the two have nothing in common: "for a slave is a living tool, just as a tool is an inanimate slave."[15]

The master possessed the power of life or death over a slave. If the slave ran away, when captured he could be killed or, at best, branded on the forehead with the letter F which stood for *fugitivus* (fugitive). A Roman writer summarized the accepted code: "Whatever a master does to a slave, undeservedly, in anger, willingly, unwillingly in forgetfulness, after careful thought, knowingly, unknowingly, is judgment, justice and law."[16]

This was Paul's world—a world of vicious immorality in which women, children, and slaves in the home suffered injustice, cruelty, and death. Against this stark background Paul wrote unusual advice to wives and husbands, children and parents, and slaves and masters.

SOME FOREIGN WORDS

Paul's inspired counsel to members of Christian households in the region of Ephesus contains several key words, words not only written in a foreign language, but also words unfamiliar in their meaning. The correct interpretation of this passage rests heavily on the contextual meaning of three words: "submit/subject" (*hupotasso*), "head" (*kephale*), and "love" (*agapao*).

One scholar notes that the very way the Greek text has been paragraphed in English versions has compounded the exegetical problem.[17] Modern translations of Ephesians 5:21-22 vary. Three versions (Amplified, ASV, NAS) indicate each verse is a separate paragraph. Four versions (Goodspeed, Phillips, TEV, TCNT) mark that a new paragraph begins at verse 22, while five versions (Berkely, Jerusalem Bible, Moffatt, NEB, RSV) do not.[18]

The question raised by the paragraphing is related to our first key word, "submit/subject." Does "Be subject [*hupotasso*] to one another out of reverence for Christ" (5:21) relate to the previous paragraph or to the passage at hand? The fact that Paul did not use any form of the word "submit/subject" in verse 22 ("Wives to your husbands as you are to the Lord") or in verse 24 ("Wives ought to be, in everything to their husbands") supports the latter. In each case, the verb found in 5:21 is implied, requiring us to link the submission of the wife in verse 22 and verse 24 to the concept of voluntary mutual submission in verse 21 (a participial form of *hupotasso*).[19]

Note also that Paul used the imperative case in his address to all five of the other family members: husbands (5:28), children (6:2), fathers (6:4), slaves (6:5), and masters (6:9). Is it possible Paul anticipated confusion over the meaning of "submission" and made these two verb omissions in order to force us to understand the word in context only? An honest interpretation of the text requires us to pay more than lip service to these verbal omissions and their importance.

Therefore, what does "submit" mean in this context? Voluntary mutual submission between husband and wife is the principle upon which Christian marriage is built. Paul's statement in 5:21 is an outflow of 5:18b, "Be filled with the Spirit." Spirit-filled living transforms the Christian home. The New Testament calls believers to be servants ("slaves") to one another without distinctions of status or sex (Gal 5:13).

In Ephesians Paul illustrates the principle of mutual submission in three areas: husband-wife (5:22-33), parent-child (6:1-4), and master-slave (6:5-9). Addressing the less powerful person in each dyad, Paul offers wives, children, and slaves hope and the possibility of transformation. In marriage mutual submission is voluntary as unto the Lord and is joined with self-sacrificing love; in parenting, it combines obedience and nurture; and in the slavery relationship, it results in a mutuality that is radically out of place in that culture.[20]

The second important but difficult word is "head" (*kephale*): "For the husband is the *head* of the wife just as Christ is *head* of the church, the body of which he is Savior" (5:23). Significant exegetical studies on the meaning of this word in the Greek language have raised questions about the uncritical equation of "head" with "authority."[21] After examining the claim that *kephale* was used in ancient Greek texts to mean "ruler or person of superior authority or rank," several scholars concluded, "There is no instance in profane Greek literature where a ruler or a hierarch is referred to as 'head' such as 'Alexander was the head of the Greek armies.'"[22] Lexicographers also give no evidence of such a meaning.[23]

The best illustration of the reluctance of the Greek language to render "head" as "authority" is in the Septuagint (LXX). In the 180 instances where the Hebrew word *ro'sh* ("leader, chief, authority") appears, the normal Greek word used is *archon* ("ruler, commander"). In only 17 places did the translators use *kephale*—5 of those have variant readings, and another 4 involve a head-tail metaphor, which leaves only 8 instances out of 180 times the LXX translators chose *kephale* for *ro'sh*.[24]

If "head" (*kephale)* did not normally mean "authority over" in Greek, what did it mean? The common Greek meaning of the word is "source, source of life, source of origin, exalted originator and completer."[25] In English we sometimes use "head" in this way when we refer to the "head" (source) of a river.

In the seven passages in the New Testament where Paul uses *kephale*, the contexts of five of them (Col 1:18; Col 2:19; Eph 4:15; 1 Cor 11:3) clearly point to this common meaning of "source."[26] The concept that "head" connotes a hierarchy with men in a role of authority over women rests largely on two passages: 1 Corinthians 11:3 and Ephesians 5:23. When we recognize one Greek meaning of *kephale* as "source" or "origin," it becomes clear Paul is not establishing a chain of command—he is establishing origins. Rather than a "ruler" over the wife, the husband is the "source" or "beginning" of woman (made from the side of Adam) even as God is the "origin" of Christ (1 Cor 11:3). "If you think 'head' means 'chief' or 'boss,'" declared Chrysostom, "you skew the godhead!"[27]

Likewise, in Ephesians 5:23 "head" is used in a head-body metaphor to show the unity of husband and wife and of Christ and the church, a common Pauline analogy. Further, where "head" is used metaphorically to represent Christ's relation to the church, it never means authority but always emphasizes Christ's servant roles as Savior, provider, and fountainhead of life.[28]

The third word, *agapao*, is more familiar to most of us. "Husbands love [*agapate*] your wives, just as Christ loved the church and gave himself up for her" (5:25). Paul repeats this admonition three more times, urging husbands to love their wives as they do their own bodies (28a) and their own selves (28b; 35). The word for love is *agape*, a distinctive type of love. The example of Christ defines the nature of *agape* love as it applies to marriage: it is a sacrificial love (25), a purifying love (26-27), a caring love (28-29), and an unbreakable love (31). "They [husbands] are not to be brutish, crude, and rude; but they are to be understanding and considerate of their wives as being persons with feelings and rights. The wife is a *person* to be loved and respected, not a *thing* to be used."[29]

As the love of the Messiah for his church is concrete, historic, and pragmatic, paid with no less price than his death, so this *agape* love is the ground and model of the concrete, historic, and pragmatic love of the husband to the wife.[30] "If he [Christ] had conducted his life according to his own best interest, there would have been no Gethsemane, no Gabbatha, no Golgotha. He gave up his own best interest and experienced the agony of Gethsemane, the agony of mistreatment at the time of his trial, and the agony of the cross. This is to be the standard by which a man judges his love for his wife."[31]

A FOREIGN WAY

The earliest disciples of Jesus were called people of "the Way" even before they were called "Christians" (Acts 9:2). The metaphor, common in Greek and Hebrew Scriptures, was used frequently of the people who walked in "God's way" or in the "way of the Lord." Jesus presented himself as "the Way" (John 14:6) and once spoke of the broad way that leads to destruction and the narrow way that leads to life (Matt 7:13-14).

"The Way" refers both to the destination of the journey and to the manner of travel. "To walk in 'the Way' involves a moral style so intimately related to the destination itself that to wander from 'the Way' is to miss the goal (a righteous life in a community faithful to God)."[32]

Into a society of vicious immorality where wealth was worshiped, life was cheap, and purity and chastity were vanishing, came a new way—a way foreign to the first-century culture. The ethical lifestyle of the first followers of "the Way" is described in the second-century *Epistle to Diognetus*: "Every foreign land is for them a fatherland and every fatherland a foreign land. They marry like the rest of men and beget children, but they do not abandon the babies that are born. They share a common board, but not a common bed."[33]

In Ephesians Paul challenged the Christian family to live by the principle of mutual yieldedness in love based upon the family's acceptance of Christ as the Lord of the home. The apostle's counsel is radically counterculture, for the Christian way "is more than a matter of a new understanding. Christianity is an invitation to be part of an alien people who make a difference because they see something that cannot otherwise be seen without Christ."[34]

The Roman culture required a woman to accept the authority of her husband, but Paul gave a new interpretation to authority and a new attitude about the marriage relationship. Christian marriage involves a mutual submission of husband and wife to each other (5:21), based on *agape* love (5:25). The analogy is that of the body. Husbands and wives are to be "one flesh" (5:31), and just as Christ loved his body (the church), so the husband in loving his wife loves himself, for she is his body (5:28). Three times Paul invokes the example of Christ to illustrate what he means. Christ put the welfare of the church over his own, even to the point of death. Christian love will make any sacrifice for the welfare of the beloved.

The unity of husband and wife is so complete that they no longer exist as separate selves, but as one (5:28-31). The Christian husband is not to act in a harsh, uncaring way toward his wife, but with tender, loving support and care. The Christian wife is to show strong respect for her husband (5:33). Through love, on the one hand, and honor on the other, husband and wife are to mirror the great mystery itself, the union between Christ and his church (5:32).

Children in the Christian household also live under the lordship of Christ and are called upon to obey their parents "in the Lord" (6:1). To "honor father and mother" was the first commandment given with a promise, as well as the first commandment each child was taught (6:2).

Addressing parents, Paul warns fathers against creating anger in children that leads to lasting bitterness and resentment (6:4a), an injunction he repeated to the Colossians, adding "lest they become discouraged" (3:21). Christian parenting is based upon "the discipline and instruction of the Lord" (6:4b); in attitude and content it reflects God's will.

Against the terrible background of slavery in the Roman Empire, Paul writes astounding advice to the Christian household. The command to "obey your earthly masters" (6:5) contains nothing new; the unique element is in the slave's attitude. Slaves should offer their slavery to the true Lord as service to him. With "fear and trembling" before the Lord, the slave should serve "with singleness of heart" (6:5b). The Christian servant was to have no mixed motives, but was to serve wholeheartedly, with enthusiasm and consistency, as unto the Lord (6:6-7). The slave's ultimate confidence rests in God's justice and not in possible rewards from earthly masters (6:8).[35]

Christian slave-owners are counseled "to do the same" (6:9), to relate to their slaves in the same spirit and with the same attitude. "Threatening" (6:9) has no place in the household of a Christian master, for as the slave must render wholehearted service, so the master's response should be kindness. The owner of slaves should also be aware that his relationship to his slave is temporary; his concern should be about his relationship to Christ, before whom both slave and master stand on level ground, for with God there is "no partiality" (6:9).

Although Paul did not visualize an imminent change in cultural structures, the ethical principles he applied to the Christian home transformed existing social relationships. Seeds were also planted that led to the eventual abolition of slavery and that continue to affect marriage and family relationships to this day. Just as we cannot use Paul's teachings to justify slavery, so we must not use Paul's words to justify a hierarchical view of marriage that relegates the wife to an inferior position.

The most constructive way to build a Christian home is for each member of the family to work at surpassing the other in love and voluntary submission. Some ask, "But when differences arise, who is the head of the house?" The answer is simple. The head of the Christian home is Christ. Christian marriage is not a struggle over power, but a covenant-commitment in which "two become one" through mutual love and consideration. +

NOTES

[1] *The Baptist Faith and Message: A Statement Adopted by the Southern Baptist Convention June 14 ,2000* (Nashville: Lifeway Christian Resources of the SBC, 2000), 21.

[2] Agnieszka Tennant, "Nuptial Agreements," *Christianity Today* 11 (March 2002): 58.

[3] Ibid., 58-65, in which an Associate Editor of *Christianity Today* outlines and explains the two models of marriage espoused by evangelical egalitarians and complementarians and the results of a recent CT survey on gender roles.

[4] James R. Beck, "Is There a Head of the House in the Home?" *Pricilla Papers* 2 (Fall 1988): 1.

[5] George W. Knight III, "Husbands and Wives as Analogues of Christ and the Church," in *Recovering Biblical Manhood & Womanhood*, eds. John Piper and Wayne Grudem (Wheaton: Crossway Books, 1991), 165-78.

[6] Malcom O. Tolbert, *Ephesians: God's New People* (Nashville: Convention Press, 1979), 116.

[7] William Barclay, *The Letters to the Galatians and Ephesians* (Philadelphia: The Westminster Press, 1956), 199-200.

[8] Ibid., 202.

[9] Adapted from Joe E. Trull, *Walking in the Way: An Introduction to Christian Ethics* (Nashville: Broadman & Holman, 1997), 184-88.

[10] Demosthenes, *Neaream,*122 (1386); quoted by Markus Barth in *The Anchor Bible: Ephesians 4–6* (New York: Doubleday & Co., 1974), 655.

[11] Charles C. Ryrie, "Women, Status of," ed. Carl F. H. Henry, *Baker's Dictionary of Christian Ethics* (Grand Rapids: Baker, 1973), 712.

[12] Barclay, *Letters,* 208.

[13] Ibid., 210.

[14] S. Angus, *The Environment of Early Christianity* (New York: Charles Scribner's, 1914), 38.

[15] Barclay, *Letters,* 213.

[16] Gaius *Institutes;* quoted in Barclay, *Letters,* 214.

[17] Beck, "Is There a Head of the House in the Home?" 61-62, who notes one of the earliest manuscripts [Vaticanus (B)] marks 5:15 to 6:9 as one paragraph, but other manuscripts tended to mark shorter paragraphs from 5:3 to 5:21, and another from 5:22 to 6:9.

[18] Ibid., 63.

[19] John Howell, *Equality and Submission in Marriage* (Nashville: Broadman Press, 1979), 57-62.

[20] Gilbert Bilezikian, "Hierarchist and Egalitarian Inculturations," *Journal of the Evangelical Theological Society* 3 (December 1987): 424-25.

[21] See "The Battle of the Lexicons," *Christianity Today* (16 January 1987): 44.

[22] Gilbert Bilezikian, *Beyond Sex Roles* (Grand Rapids: Baker Book House, 1990), 215-52.

[23] Berkeley and Alvera Mickelsen in "The 'Head' of the Epistles," *Christianity Today* (20 February 1981): 20. The comprehensive lexicon of the Greek language compiled by Liddell, Scott, Jones, and McKenzie lists nearly twenty-five possible meanings of *kephale* ("head"), but does not include our common English usage of "authority over," "leader," "director," or "superior." The commonly used lexicon of Arndt and Gingrich also gives little or no support for such a meaning.

[24] Ibid., 21.

[25] Berkeley and Mickelsen, "The 'Head,'" 21-22; Bilezikian, *Beyond Sex Roles,* 23.

[26] Berkeley and Mickelsen, "The 'Head,'" 22. See also Richard S. Cervin, "Does *kephale* ('head') Mean 'Source' or 'Authority Over' in Greek Literature?: A Rebuttal," doctoral paper, University of Illinois, published by Christians for Biblical Equality, St. Paul MN.

[27] Joannis Chrysostom, *S. P. N. Joannis Chrysostomi, Archiepiscopi Constantinopolitani, Opera Omnia Quae Existant,* Patrologiae Cursus Completus, Series Graece, ed. J. P. Migne, no. 61 (Paris: Apud Garnier Fratres, 1862), 215-16.

[28] Bilezikian, "Hierarchist and Egalitarian Inculturations," 424.

[29] Frank Stagg, *New Testament Theology* (Nashville: Broadman Press, 1962), 298.

[30] Barth, *Anchor Bible,* 700.

[31] Ray Summers, *Ephesians: Pattern for Christian Living* (Nashville: Broadman Press, 1960), 123.

[32] Bruce Birch and Larry Rasmussen, *Bible & Ethics in the Christian Life* (Minneapolis: Augsburg, 1989), 22.

[33] Anonymous *Epistle to Diognetus,* v-vi, cited by Waldo Beach and H. Richard Niebuhr in *Christian Ethics* (New York: Ronald Press, 1955), 68.

[34] Stanley Hauerwas and William Willimon, *Resident Aliens* (Nashville: Abingdon Press, 1989), 24.

[35] Tolbert, *Ephesians,* 125.

CHAPTER ELEVEN

Women Leaders in the Church

Karen G. Massey

S ince the founding of the Southern Baptist Convention (SBC) in 1845, a debate has existed concerning women's leadership roles in the church. Can women serve in positions of authority? Can women be deacons? Can women teach men? Can women be ministers? While such questions have been posed and debated *ad infinitum*, it is interesting to note that Southern Baptists were more open to women serving as deacons and church leaders in the early days of the denomination than they are today.

EARLY SOUTHERN BAPTIST HISTORY

Baptist church historian Leon McBeth provides some of the most concise accounts of Southern Baptists' attitudes toward women in the early years of the denomination. In his book *Women in Baptist Life*, McBeth states that the architects of the SBC were advocates for women deacons. It should be noted that most of those advocates were men.[1] For example, R. B. C. Howell published a book in 1846 titled *The Deaconship, Its Nature, Qualifications, Relations and Duties*, in which he showed from the New Testament that early churches had deaconesses, citing Scripture from Roman 16:1, 1 Timothy 5:1-10, and 1 Timothy 3:11.[2] He concludes his study of Scripture by stating: "Take all these passages together, and I think it will be difficult for us to resist the conclusion that the word of God authorizes, and in some sense, certainly by implication, enjoins the appointment of deaconesses in the churches of Christ . . . . Deaconesses, therefore, are everywhere as necessary as they were in the days of the apostles."[3]

In 1865, Samuel Boykin, editor of the Baptist paper of Georgia, wrote an editorial on "Female Influence in the Churches—Woman's Position."[4] Boykin declared that some Baptists have so "emphasized the Pauline restrictions upon women that they have missed the positive side of the biblical message, and women have been in effect sidelined in the churches. Thus, has a mighty arm of strength been paralyzed, and a talent hidden so long that the churches are incredulous as to its real existence."[5]

Another leader in Southern Baptist life, J. R. Graves, endorsed the notion of women deacons. Graves, once called "the most influential Southern Baptist who ever lived,"[6] was the founder of the ultraconservative Landmark movement of the nineteenth century. It is ironic that the founder of such an ultraconservative movement would support women as deacons! In an article on "Women's Work in the Church," Graves wrote, "There is no doubt in the minds of Biblical and ecclesiastical scholars, that in the apostolic churches women occupied the office of the deaconship . . . . Phoebe was a deaconess of the church in Cenchrea." Graves went on to say that "There is no good reason why saintly women should not fill the office of deaconess today in most churches. In fact, they often perform the duties of the offices without the name."[7]

It is also recorded that, in the early years of the SBC, many churches had begun to ordain women as deacons. One of the most prominent of those churches was the First Baptist Church of Waco, Texas. In 1877, this church set aside six female deacons.[8] Dr. B. H. Carroll was pastor of the church at that time, and he later became the founder and first president of Southwestern Baptist Theological Seminary.[9] Other churches cited by McBeth as having long histories of women deacons include the Third Baptist Church of St. Louis, Missouri; Wake Forest Baptist Church in Winston-Salem, North Carolina; and the First Baptist Church of Decatur, Georgia. McBeth's research indicates that in the nineteenth century many Southern Baptist churches approved the office of deaconess and believed that role to be biblically based.

RECENT SOUTHERN BAPTIST PRACTICE

Unfortunately, by the middle of the twentieth century, the acceptance of women as deacons began to decline. A Baptist historian, Charles DeWeese, studied this phenomenon and concluded that changes in the role of the diaconate were responsible for this decline. DeWeese stated that in the early years the role of the deacon and deaconess was to minister to the needs of people.

But over time, the role of the deacon began to shift from ministry to administration. DeWeese concluded that "the diaconal function began to be viewed more and more in administrative, business, and management categories to the neglect of the more caring and supporting ministries."[10] As a result, fewer women were put into the role of deacon because, in American society at large, women were not generally involved in management positions.

While this decline in the leadership roles of women was disappointing, by the early 1970s there was a resurgence among Baptist churches in the ordination of women deacons. McBeth says that while the exact numbers cannot be known, "it was estimated in 1973 that two to three hundred Southern Baptist churches had women deacons or deaconesses."[11]

Sadly, the growth in numbers of women deacons in the 1970s was only temporary. By the end of the decade, the fundamentalist movement in the Southern Baptist Convention was on the rise, thus paving the way for what has been called the Southern Baptist Controversy. While the fundamentalist movement purported to focus solely on biblical authority, other issues also received attention. Although not always of first concern, near the center of the controversy was the role of women in the church. At the 1973 Convention, a resolution was passed that was titled "On the Place of Women in Christian Service."[12] This resolution made reference to "the distinctive roles of men and women in the church and in the home" and suggested that missions promotion and education were areas of service suitable for women. The resolution also stated that the Bible was "explicitly clear" on this subject, and reference was made to "God's order of authority," namely, Christ the head of every man, man the head of woman, and children in subjection to parents.[13] Similar resolutions that spoke against women's ordination and female leadership in the church were passed in subsequent years.

The attitude of the SBC concerning women in roles of authority became quite clear, and agencies and state conventions began acting accordingly. The Central Baptist Association in Oklahoma refused to seat the messengers from the First Baptist Church in Oklahoma City because the church had ordained three women deacons.[14] The Baptist General Convention of Oklahoma withdrew its invitation to a minister from Nashville when they discovered his church had ordained a woman as deacon.[15] The SBC Home Mission Board hired a pastor and then recommended he resign when the Board detected that his church had several female deacons.[16] These instances indicate that the ordination of women "had become symbolic of the division facing the Convention."[17] Frederick Schmidt summarized, "In spite of the

Convention's congregational tradition, however, the resolutions passed over the last decades have proven that it is not only prepared to legislate against the ordination of women, but is, in fact, capable of exercising some measure of real control over this issue as well."[18] As a result of the controversy in the SBC over the last twenty-five years, the numbers of women in significant leadership positions in the churches have declined significantly. While exact numbers cannot be determined, it is widely believed that very few Southern Baptist churches now have women deacons.

THE PRESENT BIBLICAL DEBATE

The debate concerning women in leadership roles in the church seems to find its basis in Scripture. While there are several scriptures that seem to support the opinions of either side of the question, there are particular verses that are vital to the issue of women deacons. These verses include 1 Timothy 3:11-12, 1 Corinthians 14:34, and 1 Timothy 2:11-12.[19]

For those who oppose the ordination of women deacons, 1 Timothy 3:11-12 (a passage describing the qualifications of deacons) is often cited as a proof text for this point of view. Verse 11 reads, "Women likewise, must be serious, not slanderers, but temperate, faithful in all things" (NRSV). Some scholars contend that Paul is referring to the "wives" of the deacons previously mentioned in verses 8-10. Those interpreters believe that the work of the deacon is of such a nature that the wives had a special role to play in supporting that work.[20]

In addition, opponents of female deacons note that verse 12 is translated in some versions "the husband of one wife" (KJV), although it reads literally *mias gunaikas andra,* "one woman man." They suggest that this verse clearly implies that deacons must be men, because it is only men who can have wives. Thus, by interpreting verses 11 and 12 in this manner, the conclusion is that only men can be deacons.

On the other hand, there are equally competent scholars who contend that 1 Timothy 3:11-12 should be interpreted in a very different way. These interpreters suggest that the two verses in no way imply that women cannot be deacons. Verse 11 can mean that Paul is referring to a group of "women" instead of "wives." The word used in this verse is *gune,* and can be translated to mean either "wives" or "women." Usually, the context of the sentence will show whether the word refers to a married woman (wife) or is a reference to the female gender (woman).

In this particular context, it seems probable that Paul is referring to a group of "women" and not "wives." Specifically, it appears that Paul is referring to a special order of women deacons. Support for this view is based upon the following: (1) the use of "likewise" in both verse 8 and verse 11, indicating a comparitive listing of requirements for another particular office in the church; (2) in the previous section describing pastors, the comparison is absent—if "wives" were meant it would seem the pastor's wives would have been described also; (3) the New Testament Greek had no special word for "deaconess," but it used the same word *diakonos* to refer to both male and female helpers in the church (cf. Rom 16:1; where Phoebe is described as a *diakonos*); and (4) if Paul had meant "wives" he would have been more explicit.[21] Church historians note that by the end of the second century there is clear evidence of female deacons in the churches.[22]

In the second passage, 1 Corinthians 14:34, it appears that Paul is encouraging women to "be silent in the churches." For those who oppose women being in positions of authority in the church, this passage is often referenced to suggest that women are to be silent and submissive in the meetings and ministry of the church. The trouble with this interpretation is that it seems clearly to contradict what Paul said earlier in 1 Corinthians 11:5. In this verse Paul clearly states that there are women in the churches who pray and prophesy, and he even offers guidelines for proper behavior for women who engage in such practices in worship. Thus, why would Paul confirm and affirm women who pray and prophesy in one instance, and then later tell them to be silent?

Those who support leadership roles for women in the church would say that 1 Corinthians 14:34 must be interpreted in light of its cultural context. In the culture of the early church, silence was an appropriate way to learn except when one had a thorough knowledge of the subject.[23] When Paul admonishes the women to be silent (v. 34), he is actually encouraging them to learn, but not by disrupting the whole assembly with unlearned questions. His encouragement to the women to learn in silence could also be an admonition to stop talking and pay attention to what was being said. This need not necessarily mean that the women were forever to remain silent.[24] There could also be a relationship between this situation at Corinth and a similar problem at Ephesus suggested in 1 Timothy 5:13. At Ephesus, many younger women were trying to teach without knowing what they were talking about.[25] Thus, Paul's admonition to the women to be silent is an admonition not to teach or speak until they themselves had been properly taught.

A third passage often used to support women's submission in the church is 1 Timothy 2:11-12. This passage clearly forbids women to teach in some sense, although most scholars agree that it forbids them only to teach in such a way as to hold authority in some form. In verse 11, women are again instructed to learn in silence but "with all submissiveness." While some scholars interpret this phrase as another Pauline injunction of female submission to male authority, others are quick to point out that the apostle did not instruct the women to be in submission to either their husbands or male church leadership.[26] While it is not clear to whom these women are to submit, some scholars suggest that this submission is to be directed toward Christ himself.[27] It is more likely, however, that Paul was suggesting that the women submit to orthodox teaching, because they had been learning from false teachers (2 Tim 3:6).[28]

In 1 Timothy 2:12, we are confronted with the question of the meaning of Paul's prohibition of women teaching. Most interpreters agree that the teaching activity referred to here (*didasko*) means the doctrinal instruction of groups of Christians.[29] Those who oppose women in positions of church leadership find in verse 12 a permanent apostolic prohibition barring all women from the official teaching office of the church. They claim that Paul's directive is in keeping with the biblical order of male headship and female submission.

Critics of this biblical interpretation claim that the argument is based on inference, noting that in the text Paul discusses an activity not an office.[30] Supporters of women leaders in the church also point out that the problem was not women teaching in general (Titus 2:3-4), or even women teaching men (2 Tim 1:5; 3:14-15), but that many women were putting themselves in the position of teachers before they had been properly taught sound doctrine.[31]

In the specific situation at Ephesus, much of the false teaching was being spread through women in the congregation. In that society the uneducated women seem to have provided the network that false teachers could use to spread their untruth (1 Tim 5:13; 2 Tim 3:6-7).[32] Thus, the most likely historical reconstruction concludes that Paul is intent on silencing the women at Ephesus because many were involved in heresy. Aida Spencer explains, "Women were learning unorthodox doctrines and probably also propagating unorthodox teachings. No wonder Paul commands they learn while not allowing them to teach."[33]

While the above are only a few examples of the scriptures used to debate the issue of women's leadership in the church, it is apparent that the Bible can be interpreted in a variety of ways based upon the cultural context of the passage, the original language in which the text was written, and the perspective of the writer of the text. Thus, Baptists could debate the role of women in the church and never reach complete agreement. Nevertheless, as Baptists who believe the Bible is God's best revelation culminated in the life and teachings of Jesus, we must continue to search the Scriptures on this subject.

Two things are becoming quite clear. First, God will continue to call women into ministries of service and leadership in the church. God's call will not be thwarted by our biases, prejudices, or ignorance. And second, as God continues to call women into ministries of leadership, administration, teaching, preaching, and service, many will continue to leave Baptist life and find homes in other denominations that affirm their gifts. How sad it is that the majority of Southern Baptists will never be graced by the full expression of women's gifts!

If indeed the Scriptures can be used to defend both sides of this issue of women leaders in the church, and if the issue will not be resolved by referencing Scripture, should we not give the "benefit of the doubt" to those women who claim God's call, women who evidence the fruits of God's calling in their lives? Could it be that the work of God's spirit is far beyond our comprehension and will not be contained by our personal misunderstandings and prejudices? +

NOTES

[1] Leon McBeth, *Women in Baptist Life* (Nashville: Broadman Press, 1979), 140.

[2] R. B. C. Howell, *The Deaconship, Its Nature, Qualifications, Relations and Duties* (Philadelphia: American Baptist Publication Society, 1846).

[3] Ibid., 104-105.

[4] *Christian Index* (13 April 1865): 2.

[5] Cited in McBeth, *Women in Baptist Life*, 141.

[6] Ibid., 142.

[7] *The Tennessee Baptist* (22 February 1879).

[8] McBeth, *Women in Baptist Life*, 143.

[9] W. W. Barnes, *The Southern Baptist Convention: 1845–1953* (Nashville: Broadman, 1954), 203-206.

[10] Charles DeWeese, "Deaconesses in Baptist History: A Preliminary Study," *Baptist History and Heritage* (January 1977): 54-55.

[11] McBeth, *Women in Baptist Life*, 145.

[12] E. Margaret Howe, *Women and Church Leadership* (Grand Rapids: Zondervan Publishing House, 1982), 143.

[13] Ibid.

[14] Nancy Ammerman, *Baptist Battles: Social Change and Religious Conflict in the Southern Baptist Convention* (New Brunswick NJ: Rutgers University Press, 1990), 94.

[15] Frederick W. Schmidt, *In a Still Small Voice: Women, Ordination, and the Church* (Syracuse NY: Syracuse University Press, 1996), 119.

[16] Ibid.

[17] Ammerman, *Baptist Battles,* 93.

[18] Schmidt, *In a Still Small Voice,* 120.

[19] For a more detailed discussion of these verses see chapter 8, "Paul: Supporter and Exhorter of Women."

[20] Thomas D. Lea and Hayne P. Griffin Jr., "First and Second Timothy," *The New American Commentary* (Nashville: Broadman Press, 1992), 119.

[21] Ibid., 119-20. Also, E. Glenn Hinson, "1-2 Timothy and Titus," *The Broadman Bible Commentary* (Nashville: Broadman Press, 1971), 319-20.

[22] Hinson, "1-2 Timothy and Titus," 320.

[23] Craig S. Keener, *Paul, Women, and Wives: Marriage and Women's Ministry in the Letters of Paul* (Peabody MA: Hendrickson Publishers, 1992), 107.

[24] Ibid., 108.

[25] Ibid.

[26] Stanley J. Grenz, *Women in the Church: A Biblical Theology of Women in Ministry* (Downers Grove IL: InterVarsity Press, 1995), 128.

[27] J. Keir Howard, "Neither Male nor Female: An Examination of the Status of Women in the New Testament," *Evangelical Quarterly* 55/1 (January 1983): 40.

[28] Grenz, *Women in the Church,* 128.

[29] Roy B. Zuck, "Greek Words for Teach," *Bibliotheca Sacra* 122 (April–June 1965): 159-60.

[30] Grenz, *Women in the Church,* 130.

[31] Ibid.

[32] Keener, *Paul, Women, and Wives,* 112.

[33] Aida Besancon Spencer, *Beyond the Curse: Women Called to Ministry* (Peabody MA: Hendrickson Publishers, 1985), 84.

CHAPTER TWELVE

Women in Christian Ministry

Fisher Humphreys

The new pastor at the church I attend in Birmingham is Sarah Jackson Shelton. Her husband is an accountant in Birmingham, and they have two young sons. Sarah's father is one of the great pastors in Alabama Baptist life, now retired. Sarah holds the M.Div. from the Southern Baptist Theological Seminary in Louisville. We were not surprised when someone told us that she had won an award for outstanding preaching while she was in seminary—she is a wonderful preacher. She is a wonderful pastor, too, a wise and compassionate person who relates beautifully to all the different kinds of people in our diverse little congregation. We learned these things about her during a twelve-month period when she served as our interim pastor.

Apparently Sarah is one of the first women to serve as pastor of a church affiliated with the Alabama Baptist State Convention. We love the Convention and its agencies such as Samford University, where I teach, and we hope the Convention will continue to accept us as members, though we expect that some people will be troubled by our having a woman as our pastor.

I suppose some people will assume that we called Sarah Shelton in order to be politically correct. Two things occur to me about that. One is that among Baptists, calling a woman as our pastor is politically incorrect, not politically correct. The other is that the phrase "politically correct" suggests that one of three things is the case: either we didn't understand the motives that led us to do what we did, or we did what we did out of a desperate need to conform to some group's expectations for us, or we're claiming we did what we did for one reason when we know we actually did it for another reason. In other words, political correctness is either stupidity, weakness, or deceit. I don't think Christians should use the phrase "politically correct." It is too laden with contempt.

We called Sarah Shelton as our pastor because we believe she has the gifts, the training, the experience, and the spirit that we need in our pastor at this time in our church's life. We believe she will be a wonderful pastor. We are grateful to God that Sarah is coming to lead us.

Still, I understand that many Christians are uncomfortable with the idea of women serving as ministers. Their view is well represented in the *2000 Baptist Faith and Message,* which says, "While both men and women are gifted for service in the church, the office of pastor is limited to men as qualified by Scripture." I think it is understandable that many Christians hold this view and think it is the biblical view.

Though I respect the sincerity, intelligence, and goodwill of such people, I do not agree with them. My purpose in this chapter is to provide a biblical argument for the church's acceptance of women serving in Christian ministry. It is the argument that has convinced me, and I hope it may be of interest to others.

There are six steps in the argument. First, I call attention to the patriarchy that characterized the world described in the Bible. Second, I identify a few women leaders in the Old and New Testaments. Third, I describe Jesus' unconventional attitude toward women. Fourth, I review two New Testament themes that support women in ministry. Fifth, I offer a theology of ordination. Finally, I respond to one of the passages that prohibit women from playing certain roles in the church.

PATRIARCHY AND THE BIBLE

The world described in the Bible was patriarchal. This is hardly surprising; apparently the entire ancient world was patriarchal. Patriarchy is a form of social organization in which fathers are the supreme authorities in their families, clans, or tribes. In a patriarchy, men possess cultural hegemony or dominance and use their dominance to exclude women from sharing in aspects of communal life. Women are expected to be submissive to men in something like the way in which, in our society today, young children are expected to be submissive to their parents.

The patriarchy of the ancient world is reflected in many ways in our Holy Scriptures. This is one of the evidences that our Bible was written by human beings. We Christians have never claimed that the Bible was written in heaven. We believe that it is God's word just as much as if it had been written in heaven. But we believe that God in infinite wisdom arranged for the word to be mediated to us through human authors; one result of this is that the patriarchal context within which the authors lived is reflected in the Bible.

But that is not all; the Bible contains passages that describe women acting as leaders in ways that challenged patriarchal assumptions.

WOMEN LEADERS IN THE BIBLE

An early example is Sarah. Her story is as much an adventure as is that of her husband, Abraham, and of course, she is as much a parent of the chosen people as is her husband. Her name means "princess," and Sarah was treasured by her husband as a princess. But for many years she had great sadness in her life, for she had no children. She was elderly when she was told that she would have a child, and she thought that was laughable; in fact, it made her laugh. When the child was born he was quite appropriately named Isaac, which means "laughter."

Another woman who broke free of ancient society's restrictions on women was Miriam, the sister of Moses and Aaron. It was Miriam who arranged for the infant Moses to be cared for by his mother after he was taken into the household of Pharaoh. During the great events of the exodus, Miriam became, along with Moses and Aaron, a religious and political leader. Centuries later, God said this to Israel: "I brought you up out of Egypt and redeemed you from the land of slavery. I sent Moses to lead you, also Aaron and Miriam" (Mic 6:4).

During the period after the death of Moses and Aaron and Miriam, when Israel was moving back into the Holy Land, the nation was led by people whom we call judges. These leaders were not only judges as we know them today, people with legal responsibilities, but were also charismatic military leaders. One of them was a woman named Deborah. Her general was named Barak, and Barak refused to go into battle unless Deborah accompanied him. Deborah led a coalition of Israelites into battle against Sisera, a leader of Canaanite forces, on the plain of Esdraelon. This was a strategic battle in Israel's control of central and northern Palestine. In addition to her work as a judge, Deborah was also a prophet (Josh 4:4).

Another woman who protected her people was Queen Esther. She was the wife of Xerxes, a king of Persia in the fifth century before Christ. Esther was Jewish, and, when she learned that the king's chief lieutenant Haman intended to kill all of the Jews in Persia, she intervened (at great personal risk) with Xerxes and succeeded in saving the Jews in Persia from extermination.

Sarah, Miriam, Deborah, and Esther played important roles in the story of salvation history that is recorded in the Hebrew Scriptures. Though these Scriptures were written in a patriarchal world, they tell about women who were called by God to act in ways that went beyond the restrictions placed on them by their society.

The same is true in the New Testament. Scattered throughout the New Testament are accounts of women exercising leadership roles and carrying out ministries in the early church. That this would happen was predicted by Peter in his great evangelistic sermon at Pentecost: "Your sons and daughters will prophesy . . . . On my servants, both men and women, I will pour out my Spirit" (Acts 2:17; Peter was quoting the prophet Joel).

In the New Testament era the Christian faith was more like a movement than an organization. Though there is a great deal that we do not know about the organizational structure of the churches of the New Testament era, it seems probable that the various churches were organized in different ways, with different officers and different functions for the various offices. As one scholar has expressed it, "There is no such thing as *the* New Testament church order."[1]

One thing we do know is this: there were women ministers in some of the New Testament churches. In Acts 18:26 we read about a couple, Priscilla and Aquila, who were teachers, and one of their students was a man. In Acts 21:8-9 we read about four unnamed women who were prophets. In Romans 16:1 we read about a woman named Phoebe who was a deacon in her church. In Philippians 4:2-3 we read about two women, Syntyche and Euodia, whom Paul describes as coworkers who have "struggled beside me in the work of the gospel." In 2 Timothy 1:5 we read about Lois and Eunice who taught the Scriptures to young Timothy. And in 1 Corinthians 11:2-16 we read that women prayed and prophesied during church services; as we would say today, they led the worship services.

In summary, given the patriarchy of the ancient world, it is not surprising that men occupy the center stage in the biblical narratives. What is surprising is that several biblical passages record the fact that women exercised leadership roles in Israel and in the churches of the New Testament era.

JESUS' ATTITUDE TOWARD WOMEN

To that surprising fact we now add another, namely, that Jesus held an unconventional attitude toward women, an attitude evident in the ways he related to them and spoke about them. I will review some of the examples of this that have been studied by Evelyn and Frank Stagg.[2]

In Mark 12:41-44 we read that Jesus praised a widow's small offering. Ironically, it was a gift she would have given in one of the outer courts of the temple, since women were not allowed to enter the inner courts.

According to John 4, Jesus engaged in a long conversation with a woman at a well in Samaria. They talked about theology, about Jesus' mission, and about her life. She accepted Jesus' message, and through her witness other Samaritans also accepted that message.

In Luke 10:38-42 we read a story about Jesus and the sisters Mary and Martha. Jesus allowed Mary to "hear his word," that is, to be a disciple, a learner of his teaching. This was in violation of the social custom that only men may become disciples of the rabbis. As the Staggs point out, "A rabbi did not instruct a woman in the Torah."[3] Today we are so accustomed to higher education being available for women as well as for men that we find it difficult to grasp the radical implications of Jesus' act. Some of us have been helped by a short story written by Isaac Singer titled "Yentl," which was made into a movie by Barbra Streisand. Certainly Jesus' contemporaries would have understood that he was doing something unconventional when he welcomed Mary as a learner, a disciple.

In Luke 8:1-3 we read that a large group of women not only benefited from Jesus' teaching but also supported him financially and accompanied him and the Twelve on evangelistic trips.

In summary, Jesus took an unconventional attitude toward women. He treated them with the same respect that he accorded to men. He expressed appreciation for their achievements. He assumed that they had the same intellectual and spiritual abilities that men have. His attitude toward women was a challenge to the assumptions of the patriarchal society in which he lived.

TWO NEW TESTAMENT TEACHINGS THAT SUPPORT WOMEN IN MINISTRY

Two important New Testament teachings are supportive of women serving as ministers in the church. One is the teaching about the priesthood of all believers, and the other is the teaching about spiritual gifts.

In the Old Testament era, priests were an elite of male descendants of Levi and later of Aaron. Two Old Testament passages, Exodus 19 and Isaiah 61, contain promises about a coming time when all of God's people would be priests. In 1 Peter 2 we read that these promises have been fulfilled in the Christian church. That Christians generally believed this truth is confirmed by five brief references to believers as priests scattered throughout the book of Revelation.

What are the biblical meanings of priesthood? What did the Hebrew priests do that other Jews did not do? There were three closely related activities: priests led worship, offered sacrifices, and offered prayers on behalf of others.

We have seen that in 1 Corinthians 11 Paul spoke of women as engaged in worship leadership. That was priestly work.

From the beginning the followers of Jesus did not offer animal sacrifices. Christians were, until the temple was destroyed in 70 AD, the only group known to us in the Roman world who did not do so, and their rationale for not doing so was extraordinary: they believed that the death of Jesus was a final sacrifice that rendered all animal sacrifices superfluous. The sacrifices that Christians offered were spiritual sacrifices (1 Pet 2:5). One spiritual sacrifice was worship itself; two others were giving money to the poor and performing acts of compassion. All three of these spiritual sacrifices are mentioned in Hebrews 13:15-16: "Through him, then, let us continually offer a sacrifice of praise to God, that is, the fruit of lips that confess his name. Do not neglect to do good and to share what you have, for such sacrifices are pleasing to God."

In Romans 12:1 Paul advised his readers to give their lives to God as living sacrifices. Offering a spiritual sacrifice is priestly work, and God calls women as well as men to that act of devotion.

Finally, the Hebrew priests offered prayers on behalf of people. This too is an activity for women as well as for men, as 1 Corinthians 11 makes clear.

In other words, all Christian churches have women priests, that is, women members who as priests are called to the priestly work of worship, sacrifice, and prayer.

The second New Testament teaching concerns spiritual gifts; the most important passages are Romans 12:3-8, 1 Corinthians 12–14, Ephesians 4:7-16, and 1 Peter 4:10-11. Paul says explicitly that all Christians are given spiritual gifts (1 Cor 12:6-7; Eph 4:6). God gives spiritual gifts to women and expects them to use their gifts in the life and ministry of the church.

The New Testament teachings about priesthood and spiritual gifts constitute a challenge to the patriarchal assumptions of the ancient world and a call to the church to welcome the ministries of women. Christian women who minister are putting into practice the unconventional attitude that Jesus had toward women, and they are following the examples of the women in the New Testament churches who were teachers, prophets, deacons, worship leaders, and coworkers with the apostles.

THE MEANING OF ORDINATION

Two other questions need to be answered: (1) What is the meaning of ordination? (2) What are we to make of the New Testament passages in which women are prohibited from playing certain roles in the life of the church?

The New Testament does not contain a doctrine of ordination. Churches in the New Testament era occasionally laid hands on individual members, and sometimes this was done as members began a new phase of ministry.[4] Across the centuries the church has continued this practice and has understood its meaning in three different ways. The Roman Catholic Church has understood ordination as conferring upon a man an indelible grace that authorizes him to conduct the Mass. Magisterial reformers such as Martin Luther and John Calvin understood ordination to confer upon a man the authority to proclaim the word of God.

These understandings of ordination are not appropriate for Baptists because Baptists believe that churches are authorized by Christ to celebrate the Lord's Supper whether or not an ordained person is present, and they believe that all Christians are responsible to give a witness to God's word.

A third understanding of ordination is that it is a church's confirmation that it concurs with a person that she or he has been called by God to perform some ministry, and a church's blessing on the individual as he or she begins that ministry. Ordination is not a conferral of authority over others, but rather a confirmation and a blessing. This is the only understanding of ordination that is appropriate for Baptists. When it is embraced, it puts to rest the objections about ordination conferring upon women an authority over men.

PASSAGES PROHIBITING WOMEN FROM PLAYING CERTAIN ROLES IN THE CHURCH

The most compelling biblical argument again women serving as ministers is, of course, the presence in the New Testament of passages in which women are prohibited from playing certain roles in the church. I believe that 1 Timothy 2 is the most forceful of these passages, so I shall give attention to it; what I say about it may be said about other similar passages.

Here is the difficult passage:

> I desire, then, that in every place the men should pray, lifting up
> holy hands without anger or argument; also that the women
> should dress themselves modestly and decently in suitable cloth-
> ing, not with their hair braided, or with gold, pearls, or expensive
> clothes, but with good works, as is proper for women who profess
> reverence for God. Let a woman learn in silence with full submis-
> sion. I permit no woman to teach or to have authority over a
> man; she is to keep silent. For Adam was formed first, then Eve;
> and Adam was not deceived, but the woman was deceived and
> became a transgressor. Yet she will be saved through childbearing,
> provided they continue in faith and love and holiness, with mod-
> esty. (1 Tim 2:8-15)[5]

I will make two simple points about this passage. First, if we apply this passage to the church today, then women should not serve as ministers in
churches. I think it is important to acknowledge this fact. Second, I think
that the principal question to be answered about the passage is this: Is this
prohibition a universal principle applicable to all times and places, or is it
rather a rule intended only for and appropriate only to the particular time
and place addressed by the author?

All Christians believe that the Bible contains principles that apply to all
times and places. An example is "You shall love the Lord your God with all
your heart" (Matt 22:37). This teaching is universal in its application rather
than culture-specific.

On the other hand, all Christians recognize that the Bible contains teachings that do not apply to all times and places. It is customary to describe these
teachings as culturally conditioned, but I do not think this is a good way to
put it, for this reason: Since we use language when we make statements, and
since language is the central component in culture, all statements are culturally
conditioned. I prefer to say that teachings that do not apply in all times and
places are "culture-specific," by which I mean that they are applicable to a particular culture but not to all cultures.

First Timothy 2 contains teachings that most Christians agree are culture-
specific. For example, it says that women should not braid their hair or wear
gold or pearls. Most Christians today regard these things as inappropriate in
Paul's world but as acceptable in today's world. The spirit behind them is pre-
sumably that Christians should be modest in their appearance.

Is the same thing true of Paul's instructions that women are not to teach or
have authority over men? Are these instructions, like those about pearls and

braided hair, culture-specific? Or are they universal? I think they are culture-specific, and I think that the universal principle that underlies them is something like this: Christians should not behave in ways that cause profound offense to the gospel and thus prevent the church from carrying out its mission to the world. In the patriarchal world of the biblical era, it would have been deeply offensive for women to teach and to exercise authority over men.

What about today? I think that there may be some societies today in which women's exercise of authority over men is so deeply offensive that the gospel cannot be heard when preached by churches in which women do these things. But in most societies today, particularly in technologically developed societies, the opposite is the case. In our culture the freedom and dignity of women are everywhere affirmed. In American society, where women are bankers, military officers, physicians, and engineers, it is deeply offensive to many people that women are excluded from leadership in churches.

If the universal principle that underlies 1 Timothy 2 is that church members should not give such profound offense to a society that the gospel cannot be heard, then in America today churches should welcome women as ministers. Why? Because in our society it is as scandalous for the church to refuse to welcome women into ministry as it would have been in the ancient world for the church to have welcomed women into all forms of ministry.

The issue concerning 1 Timothy 2 is not whether we believe the Bible but how we interpret it. God is sovereign, which means, among other things, that God is free to arrange the church's life in any way God likes; God is free to call men into ministry and not women, and God is free to call both women and men into ministry. Our responsibility as members of the church is not to choose a practice we happen to like, but to seek God's will and then to attempt to do it.

I believe it is God's will for women to serve as ministers of the church in developed societies today. In these societies women leaders do not give grave offense to the gospel, and the work of the church will prosper if the church adopts Jesus' attitudes toward women and follows the example of the women prophets and deacons and worship leaders whose ministries are named in the New Testament.

St. Irenaeus has written, *Glorio dei homo vivens*—"the glory of God is a human being who is fully alive."[6] It is God's will is for all people to experience wholeness and fullness of life. One of the most egregious contributors to human impoverishment and alienation is the systemic, invidious diminishment of women in patriarchies. I believe that the diminishment of women is weakening, and I believe that the future for women is a bright one, because I believe God intends for women to experience life in all its fullness. Therefore I believe that we Christians may hope for a better future and that we may move into the future with joy and confidence in God. ✦

NOTES

[1] Eduard Schweizer, *Church Order in the New Testament* (London: SCM Press Ltd., 1959), 13.

[2] Evelyn and Frank Stagg, *Woman in the World of Jesus* (Philadelphia: The Westminster Press, 1978), chs. 4 and 5.

[3] Ibid., 118.

[4] See, for examples, Acts 6:6; 13:3; 1 Timothy 4:14; 2 Timothy 1:6.

[5] For a more intensive study of this passage, see chapter 8.

[6] Irenaeus, *Against Heresies* 4, 20, 6, in Henry Bettenson, ed., *The Early Christian Fathers* (London: Oxford University Press, 1963), 104.

Sheri Adams has been Professor of Church History and Theology at the M. Christopher White School of Divinity at Gardner-Webb University since 1995, before which she taught with her husband Bob at the Seminario Internacional Teologico Bautista in Buenos Aires, Argentina. A graduate of Northeast Louisiana State University (B.M.E.), Louisiana State University (M.Ed.), and New Orleans Baptist Theological Seminary (M.Div.; Th.D.), she has authored *What the Bible Really Says About Women*, and she presently is Academic Network Coordinator for Global Women.

Ruth Ann Foster is Associate Professor of Christian Scriptures at George W. Truett Seminary at Baylor University, where she began as a founding faculty member in 1994. Previously she was Minister of Education at Manor Baptist in San Antonio. A graduate of Clear Creek Baptist College in Kentucky (B.Th.) and Southwestern Baptist Theological Seminary (M.Div.; Ph.D.), she has published numerous articles and is a frequent speaker for churches and conferences. In 1998 Dr. Foster was named Outstanding Faculty Member, one of eight in the entire Baylor University faculty.

William E. Hull is Research Professor at Samford University in Birmingham, where he received his Bachelor's degree. He earned the M.Div. and Ph.D. degrees from The Southern Baptist Theological Seminary and did advanced study at the University of Goettingen, Germany, and Harvard University. At Southern he served as professor in the New Testament Department, Dean of the School of Theology, and Provost (1969–1975). In 1987, Dr. Hull returned to Samford. Author of five books on theology, he has also written numerous chapters and articles in scholarly publications. Since 1991 he has served as Minister-in-Residence at Mountain Home Baptist Church.

Fisher Humphreys is Professor of Divinity at the Beeson Divinity School of Samford University. He holds degrees from Mississippi College (B.A.), Loyola Universitly (M.A.), Oxford University (M.Litt.), and New Orleans Baptist Theological Seminary (B.D.; Th.D.), where he served as editor of the

Theological Educator. He is the author of several books including *Thinking About God: An Introduction to Christian Theology* and the latest, *The Way We Were: How Southern Baptist Theology Has Changed and What It Means To Us All.*

Dan Gentry Kent was Professor of Old Testament, Southwestern Baptist Theological Seminary, from which he received the M.Div. and Th.D. degrees. A graduate of Baylor University (B.A.), he has done additional study at Oxford University. The author of several Bible study books, he was also editor of the *Southwestern Journal of Theology* for nine years. Dan served as Chair of the Board of Directors of Christians for Biblical Equality and is now President of the Baptist History and Heritage Society.

Catherine Clark Kroeger is Adjunct Associate Professor of Classical and Ministry Studies at Gordon-Conwell Theological Seminary in Massachusetts. A Ph.D. graduate in classical area studies from the University of Minnesota, from which she also earned an M.A. in Greek, she received her B.A. from Bryn Mawr College. She is founder of Christians for Biblical Equality and author and editor of numerous articles and books (i.e., *I Suffer Not a Woman,* co-authored with her husband Richard; *Study Bible for Women;* and *The IVP Women's Bible Commentary*). Widely heard as a speaker and conference leader, she also serves as Bible teacher and deacon at Brewster Baptist Church near her home on Cape Cod.

Gladys S. Lewis has been Professor of English at the University of Central Oklahoma since 1990, after serving with her husband Wilbur, a surgeon, as an SBC missionary in South America. A graduate of Texas Christian University (B.A.), she also completed one year of study at Southwestern Baptist Theological Seminary in preparation for mission service, and later earned degrees at Central State University (M.A.) and Oklahoma State University (Ph.D.). Dr. Lewis is author of a large number of articles, reviews, and books whose themes range from religious to medical to academic. She is presently at work on *The Biblical Key to Uncle Tom's Cabin: The Authority of Rhetoric.*

Karen G. Massey is Assistant Professor of Christian Education and Faith Development at the McAfee School of Theology, Mercer University. Previously she served as associate pastor of Northside Drive Baptist Church in Atlanta. A graduate of the University of Georgia (B.S.Ed.) and The Southern Baptist Theological Seminary (M.A.; Ph.D.), she has done graduate studies at Harvard and Boston College, and she is presently National President of Baptist Women in Ministry.

Julie Pennington-Russell has served as pastor of Calvary Baptist Church in Waco, Texas, since 1998, previously serving as pastor and associate pastor at Nineteenth Avenue Baptist Church in San Francisco from 1984 to 1998. She received a B.A. from the University of Central Florida, a M.Div. from Golden Gate Baptist Theological Seminary, and will enter the D.Min. program at Baylor's Truett Seminary in 2003.

Audra E. Trull is assistant to the editor of the bimonthly journal *Christian Ethics Today*. A graduate of the University of Texas (B.S.), she has also studied at Southwestern Baptist Theological Seminary. An elementary teacher for twenty years, she has led church conferences and written journal articles. Audra also assists her husband in the development of a new church at Driftwood, Texas, where she is the teacher of adults.

Joe E. Trull is editor of *Christian Ethics Today*, adjunctive teacher at Wayland Baptist University (San Antonio) and Baylor University, and pastor of the baptist church of Driftwood. While Professor of Christian Ethics at New Orleans Baptist Theological Seminary from 1985 to 1999, he authored two textbooks: *Walking in the Way: An Introduction to Christian Ethics* and *Ministerial Ethics* (co-author), as well as numerous articles. A graduate of Oklahoma Baptist University (B.A.) and Southwestern Baptist Theological Seminary (M.Div.; Th.D.), he was also pastor of churches in Oklahoma, Texas, and Virginia (1960–1985).

Charles Wellborn is Distinguished Professor of Religion Emeritus, Florida State University, and for twenty years was Dean of the Overseas Campus in London where he now lives. A graduate of Baylor University (B.A.; M.A.), Southwestern Baptist Theological Seminary (Th.M.), and Duke University (Ph.D.), he was twice National Champion Debater while in college. Widely known for his numerous books and articles, for ten years he was pastor of the Seventh and James Baptist Church in Waco, Texas. Among his books is *Grits, Grace, and Goodness.*

SUGGESTIONS FOR FURTHER READING

Adams, Sheri. *What the Bible Really Says About Women.* Macon GA: Smyth & Helwys, 1994.

Bilezikian, Gilbert. *Beyond Sex Roles.* Grand Rapids: Baker Book House, 1985.

Bristow, John Temple. *What Paul Really Said About Women.* San Francisco: HarperCollins, 1988.

Grenz, Stanley J. with Denise Muirkjesbo. *Women in the Church: A Biblical Theology of Women in Ministry.* Downers Grove: InterVarsity Press, 1995.

Groothuis, Rebecca Merrill. *Good News for Women: A Biblical Picture of Gender Equality.* Grand Rapids: Baker Books, 1997.

————. *Women Caught in the Conflict: The Culture War between Traditionalism and Feminism.* Grand Rapids: Baker Books, 1994.

Jewett, Paul. *Man as Male and Female.* Grand Rapids: Eerdmans, 1975.

Kroeger, Catherine Clark, and Mary J. Evans, editors. *The IVP Women's Bible Commentary.* Downers Grove: InterVarsity Press, 2002.

Kroeger, Catherine Clark, and Richard Clark. *I Suffer Not a Woman: Rethinking 1 Timothy 2:11-15 in Light of Ancient Evidence.* Grand Rapids: Baker Book House, 1982.

McBeth, Leon. *Women in Baptist Life.* Nashville: Broadman Press, 1979.

Myers, Carol, general editor. *Women in Scripture: A Dictionary of Named and Unnamed Women in the Hebrew Bible, The Apocryphal/Deuterocanonical Books, and the New Testament.* Grand Rapids, Eerdmans, 2000.

Priscilla Papers. Carol Thiessen, editor. A Quarterly Journal Published by the Christians for Biblical Equality, 122 W. Franklin Ave., Suite 218, Minneapolis, MN 55404.

Spencer, Aida Besancon. *Beyond the Curse: Women Called to Ministry.* New York: Thomas Nelson, 1985.

Stagg, Evelyn, and Frank Stagg. *Women in the World of Jesus.* Philadelphia: Westminster Press, 1978.

Trull, Joe E. *Walking in the Way: An Introduction to Christian Ethics.* Nashville: Broadman & Holman, 1997, chapter 8, "Human Equality: Gender and Race."

Tucker, Ruth. *Women in the Maze: Questions & Answers on Biblical Equality.* Downers Grove: InterVarsity Press, 1992.

Tucker, Ruth A., and Walter L. Liefeld. *Daughters of the Church: Women and Ministry from New Testament Times to the Present.* Grand Rapids: Zondervan, 1987.

SMYTH&HELWYS
PUBLISHING, INCORPORATED • MACON, GEORGIA